Interrupted Identity

Interrupted Identity

How to Guard Against & Recover From Having Your Identity Stolen

Ron G. Patton

Writers Club Press
San Jose New York Lincoln Shanghai

Interrupted Identity
How to Guard Against & Recover From Having Your Identity Stolen

Library of Congress Card Number: 00-107356

Published by Writers Club Press
an imprint of iUniverse.com, Inc.

For information address:
iUniverse.com, Inc.
620 North 48th Street
Suite 201
Lincoln, NE 68504-3467
www.iuniverse.com

ISBN: 0-595-12803-3

Printed in the United States of America

Contents

Foreword

Recently, an article appeared in my local newspaper about the latest insidious crime to hit the streets—identity theft. Who would ever think of having someone stealing the most intimate aspect of their life, their very identity? I certainly never had, at least not until I attended a conference recently, and saw a fraud examiner demonstrate how easy it is to be victimized in this way.

Cases of identity theft have increased from less than 50,000 in 1992 to more than half a million in 1997, according to watchdog groups. With the burgeoning Internet use, the potential for identity theft is rising exponentially. To add insult to injury, victims of identity theft have reported that they've received little or no help from the police or credit card companies, and they have been forced to spend hundreds of hours and sometimes thousands of dollars in damage control after someone has obtained their social security number or other personal information to help them perpetrate a fraud.

You are about to delve into some important areas that, if you did the research yourself, would take an investment of many, many hours. With *Interrupted Identity*, Ron Patton has come up with some solutions to a problem that never has to cost you the time, aggravation, and money that so many people are having to spend to combat. In the more than ten years that I've known Ron, I've often been amazed at his tireless efforts in educating consumers about their rights and showing them how to deal with their troublesome legal situations. In fact, when I've needed "how-to" answers to various legal questions, he always has a mountain of "self-help" information to share. He is also a well-qualified handwriting expert who is experienced in understanding what makes people tick.

Reading *Interrupted Identity* has been a real eye-opener for me, and I know it will be for you, too. You will learn about the laws that have been enacted to protect you and how to use them, as well as many other valuable resources. Ron will tell you what to steps to take if your identity has been stolen, and even gives you actual forms to use.

The information contained in this book will become ever-more timely as the Information Age advances and the world continues to shrink. *Interrupted Identity* could mean the difference between wondering whether an identity thief will come after your personal information, and relaxing in the knowledge that you have outsmarted him before he gets started.

Sheila R. Lowe, FACFE

Court-qualified handwriting expert and

author of *The Complete Idiot's Guide to Handwriting Analysis*

Introduction

No one has precise statistics, mainly because identity theft (fraud) can go for years before it's discovered. However, everyone seems to agree that identity fraud has become epidemic. Here are some shocking statistics illustrating this—

❖ In 1995, the Financial Crimes Division of the Secret Service made a total of 9,470 arrests, of which 8,806 (93 percent) involved identity fraud.

❖ According to Social Security Administration Officials, the number of "SSN misuse" (identity fraud) investigations increased from 305 in 1996 to 1,153 in 1997.

❖ In 1993, the IRS detected a total of 5,438 identity fraud schemes, consisting of 77,840 questionable tax returns that claimed a total of $137 million in refunds.

❖ Trans Union reported that the number of consumer inquiries to its Fraud Victim Assistance Department rose from 35,235 in 1992 to 522,922 in 1997.

❖ According to the American Bankers Association, in 1997, the average number of stolen credit cards reported for each of the 10 large banks surveyed was 112,730. The average number of credit-card fraud categories in 1996 for *each* large bank was 16,801.

❖ In 1997, the Internet Fraud Watch received a total of 1,152 reports of possible Internet fraud, representing a threefold increase over 1996. (Note: The Internet fraud Watch was created in 1996 by the

National Consumers League to operate work with the League's National Fraud Information Center).

❖ There are currently more than one million web pages on the Internet that will show you how and where to get fake I.D.s. (search conducted at **www.altavista.com**).

Creditors you never heard of…

Your new Visa, MasterCard or other credit card never reaches your mailbox. Sometime later, creditors you never heard of are constantly writing and telephoning you demanding payment for goods and services you never purchased. Your credit history, once perfect, is no longer. Now, you are being denied financing (credit) due to several past due *late pays* appearing on your credit report. How could this possibly be happening to you? Unfortunately, it could and it has to as many as 500,000 victims each year. This crime, known as *identity theft* is the fasting growing crime in America. But, other types of fraud, such as: Internet fraud, tele-com fraud and insurance fraud are also growing rapidly.

The 1990's gave birth to a new type of crooks called identity thieves. Their tools are your everyday transactions. Each transaction requires you to share personal information: your bank and credit card account numbers; your income; your Social Security number (SSN); and your name, address and phone numbers. An identity thief steals some piece of your personal information and adapts it without your knowledge to commit fraud or theft. An all-too-common example is when an identity thief uses your personal information to open a credit card account in your name, then "maxes" it out with numerous charges.

While, most of this information has always been in the public record, access to it has been limited to those individuals who are familiar with complicated county court records. Now that this information can be found on the Internet, anyone with a computer and Internet access can readily obtain this information. Thus, information previously not commonly available to the criminal element is now just a keystroke away.

This book will examine what identity theft is, how it happens, why you should be concerned, how to avoid credit identity theft and what to do if someone steals your credit identity.

Chapter One

What is Identity Theft?

That which has always been accepted by everyone, everywhere, is almost certain to be false.
—Paul Valery, 1871–1945

There is no one universally accepted definition of identity fraud. Typically, identity fraud refers to the illegal use of personal identifying information—such as name, address, Social Security Number (SSN), and date of birth—to commit financial fraud. Identity fraud can incorporate a host of crimes, ranging from the unauthorized use of a credit card to a comprehensive takeover of another person's identity and financial accounts. In short, an identity thief can fraudulently use personal identifying information to take over a person's identity and open new accounts. He can also apply for loans, credit cards, and social benefits; rent apartments and establish services with utility companies; and engage in many other types of fraudulent activities, which can result in the loss of assets or creditworthiness.

Identity Theft can claim many victims. Credit grantors, such as banks and retail merchants, can be victims because they finance the selling of goods and services that ultimately are not paid for. The individuals whose identities are stolen are victims, too, even though they may be protected in some instances from personal financial loss—e.g., by insurance coverage or credit card maximum-loss and/or reimbursement provisions.

Even if they have no out-of-pocket costs, individual victims can nonetheless suffer from injuries to their reputations and must undergo a sometimes very lengthy and agonizing process of clearing up their

3

credit history. A *Washington Post* article described a situation where an individual had his wallet stolen and his identity later compromised. The criminal who stole the wallet was later caught for committing additional crimes. When questioned by the authorities, the criminal identified himself as the individual from whom he had stolen the wallet, and he had the identification to prove it. A criminal record was established for the criminal in the original victim's name. As a result, of this criminal record the victim suffered numerous problems, including repeated rejections by potential employers. In the meantime, other victims may be unable to obtain a home mortgage, or secure other time-critical loans, such as tuition loans for college-age children.

Chapter Two

How Does One's Identity Get Stolen?

Pay attention to your enemies, for they are the first to discover your mistakes.
                                    —Antisthenes, c.445–c.365 B.C.

Despite your best efforts to manage the flow of your personal information or to keep it to yourself, skilled identity thieves may use a variety of methods — low- and hi-tech to gain access to your data. Here are some of the ways impostors can get your personal information and take over your identity:

❖ They obtain personal information through property deeds and court case data such as, unlisted telephone numbers, social security numbers, physical description (height, weight, etc.). This information is made available to brokers, who in turn sell it to interested parties.

❖ They steal wallets and purses containing your identification and credit and bankcards.

❖ They steal your mail, including your bank and credit card statements, pre-approved credit offers, telephone calling cards and tax information.

❖ They complete a "change of address form" to divert your mail to another location.

❖ They rummage through your trash, or the trash of businesses, for personal data in a practice known as "Dumpster diving."

There is even a how-to video being marketed called *The Ultimate Dive* claiming that anyone can learn how to dumpster dive!

❖ They fraudulently obtain your credit report by posing as a landlord, employer or someone else who may have a legitimate need for and a legal right to the information.

❖ They get your business or personnel records at work.

❖ They find personal information in your home.

❖ They buy your personal information from "inside" sources. For example, an identity thief may pay a store employee for information about you that appears on an application for goods, services or credit.

❖ They use personal information you share on the Internet.

Use these steps to safely surf in private:

1. On your browser's *preference menu*, select not to accept *cookies*—those small files keeping track of your surfing habits and default settings at specific sites—or at least have your browser prompt you before accepting them.

If you want to see what information is stored in your cookie file, use a text editor or word processor to open a file called *cookie.txt* or *MagicCookie* in your browser's folder or directory.

Of course, there is a way you can delete cookies. Here's how:

Your cookies are saved to a simple text file that you can delete as you please, whether you use Netscape or Microsoft Internet Explorer (MSIE).

In order to do this properly; remember to close your browser first. This is because all your cookies are held in memory until you close your browser. So, if you delete the file with your browser open, it will make a new file when you close it and your cookies will be back.

Remember that deleting your cookie file entirely will cause you to "start from scratch" with every web site you usually visit. So, it may be preferable to open the cookies.txt file (in the case of Netscape) and remove only the entries you don't like, or go to the cookies folder (in the case of MSIE) and delete the files from servers you don't want.

A worthwhile website on cookies is aptly called **www.cookiecentral.com.** Here you can read about everything there is to know about Internet Cookies. It even has a regularly updated section on its website called *the Unofficial Cookie FAQ* where all your cookie questions are answered.

Another website to visit is **www.myprivacy.org.** This site is dedicated to online privacy issues and online personalization. When you visit this site, they won't collect any information about you. You remain anonymous to them. You can email your questions to **comments@myprivacy.org.**

2. If you're using your credit cards online more frequently, print and save all receipts from web transactions. Then, check them against your monthly statements. Additionally, use a separate card, preferably one with a low credit line, for online shopping;

3. Avoid public newsgroups, and mailing lists. However, if you must involve yourself with these, create separate, multiple e-mail addresses to use for these , which are available for free. By using a mail forwarding service, you can receive mail at a special address, but it doesn't necessarily let you send it from that address. However, some services do provide a Web interface for that. Go to **www.anonymizer.com,** or **www.enonymous.com** for a listing of reliable anonymous e-mail forwarding services. You can also find more free e-mail service by contacting one of the following:

    a.   *Anonymous.to* (**http://anonymous.to/**). You can send anonymous messages via this site as their remailer strips off all email headers so that no originating information is available.

b. *PrivacyX* (**www.privacyx.com**) PrivacyX offers a free anonymous digital certificate that you can use to make your web browsing anonymous. They offer a free anonymous email service that includes the option of sending encrypted messages.

c. *Replay* (**http://replay.com/remailer**) The anonymous remailer services at Replay will hide your identity effectively. You have a choice of email-based and SSL server remailers.

d. The *Free Email Address Directory* (**www.emailaddresses.com**). This is a well-organized index of dozens of services, arranged by service type;

e. *DejaNews* (**www.dejanews.com/rg_reg.xp**). This offers a good Usenet reader, plus Web-based e-mail.

f. *HotMail* (**www.hotmail.com**).

g. *Yahoo Mail* (**http://mail.yahoo.com**).

Identity thieves can use your personal information in the following ways:

1. They call your credit card issuer and, pretending to be you, ask to change the mailing address on your credit card account. The impostor then runs up charges on your account. Because your bills are being sent to the new address, it may take some time before you realize there's a problem.

2. They open a new credit card account, using your name, date of birth and SSN. When they use the credit card and don't pay the bills, the delinquent account is reported on your credit report.

3. They establish phone or wireless service in your name.

4. They open a bank account in your name and write bad checks on that account.

5. They file for bankruptcy under your name to avoid paying debts they've incurred under your name, or to avoid eviction.
6. They counterfeit checks or debit cards, and drain your bank account.
7. They buy cars by taking out auto loans in your name.

Chapter Three

How You Can Avoid Having Your Identity Stolen

There are many things that we would throw away, if we were not afraid that others might pick them up.

Oscar Wilde, 1854–1900

What happens to the personal information you provide to companies, marketers and government agencies? They may use your information just to process your order. They may use it to create a profile about you and then let you know about products, services or promotions. Or they may share your information with others. More organizations are offering consumers choices about how their personal information is used. For example, many let you "opt out" of having your information shared with others or used for promotional purposes.

You can learn more about the choices you have to protect your personal information from credit bureaus, state Departments of Motor Vehicles and direct marketers.

Credit Bureaus

Pre-Screened Credit Offers

In 1998, the credit card industry mailed out over 3 billion pre-approved offers of credit to Americans. The industry didn't even bother verifying the applicants' identities. Thus, a lot of impostors got valid credit cards. If you don't accept those pre-screened credit card offers in the mail, here's how to handle them: shred them completely instead of just tearing them up. Otherwise, identity thieves may retrieve the offers for their own use without your knowledge.

To opt out of receiving pre-screened credit card offers, call **1-888-5-OPTOUT (1-888-567- 8688)**. The three major credit bureaus use the same toll-free number to let consumers choose not to receive pre-screened credit offers.

Marketing Lists

The credit bureaus admittedly sell *credit headers*—the top portion of credit reports—without consent. They earn millions of dollars in doing so. Each credit header has the following information: (1) consumer's name; (2) address and phone number (including *unlisted* ones); (3) mother's maiden name; (4) birthdate; and (5) Social Security Number.

Of the three major credit bureaus, only Experian offers consumers the opportunity to have their names removed from lists that are used for marketing and promotional purposes. To have your name removed from Experian's marketing lists, call **1-800-407-1088**.

Departments of Motor Vehicles

Take a look at your driver's license. All the personal information on it — and more — is on file with your state Department of Motor Vehicles (DMV). It appears that numerous departments of motor vehicle agencies (DMVs) provide personal information in the form of mailing lists. For a fee, DMVs conduct customized searches of driver's license and car registration records, which often contain detailed personal data including unlisted addresses and medical conditions. According to a *Washington Post* article, one state agency earned approximately $12.9 million in revenue in exchange for motor vehicle agency generated mailing list information.

However, a state DMV may distribute your personal information for law enforcement, driver safety or insurance underwriting purposes, but you may have the right to choose not to have the DMV distribute your personal information for other purposes, including for direct marketing.

Not every DMV distributes personal information for direct marketing or other purposes. You may be able to opt out if your state DMV distributes personal information for these purposes. Contact your state DMV for more information. As of this writing, not all states allow you this opt-out option pursuant to the *Federal Driver's Privacy Protection Act* , which states in general that:

(b) a State department of motor vehicles, and any officer, employee, or contractor, thereof, shall not knowingly disclose or otherwise make available to any person or entity personal information about any individual obtained by the department in connection with a motor vehicle record.

As of this writing, the following states allow you this opt-out option:

Alaska
Arizona
Colorado
Connecticut
Delaware
Florida
Idaho
Iowa
Kansas
Kentucky
Louisiana
Maine
Maryland
Michigan
Minnesota
Mississippi

Missouri
Montana
Nebraska
New-Hampshire
New-York
North-Carolina
North-Dakota
Ohio
Oregon
Rhode Island
South Dakota
Tennessee
West Virginia —Online opt-out.
Wisconsin
Wyoming

Direct Marketers

The Direct Marketing Association's (DMA) Mail, E-mail and Telephone Preference Services allow consumers to opt out of direct mail marketing, e-mail marketing and/or telemarketing solicitations from many national companies. Because your name will not be on their lists, it also means that these companies can't rent or sell your name to other companies.

To remove your name from many national direct mail lists, write:

DMA Mail Preference Service
P.O. Box 9008
Farmingdale, NY 11735-9008

To remove your e-mail address from many national direct e-mail lists, visit **www.e-mps.org**

To avoid unwanted phone calls from many national marketers, send your name, address, and telephone number to:

DMA Telephone Preference Service
P.O. Box 9014
Farmingdale, NY 11735-9014

For more information, visit **www.the-dma.org**

Reducing Your Risk

While you probably can't prevent identity theft entirely, you can reduce your risk. By managing your personal information wisely, cautiously and with an awareness of the issue, here's how you can help guard against identity theft:

❖ Before you reveal any personally identifying information, find out how it will be used and whether it will be shared with others. Ask if you have a choice about the use of your information: can you choose to have it kept confidential?

❖ Pay attention to your billing cycles. Follow up with creditors if your bills don't arrive on time. A missing credit card bill could mean an identity thief has taken over your credit card account and changed your billing address to cover his tracks. If this is the case, close the account. When opening a new account, ask that a password is used before any inquiries or changes can be made on the account.

❖ Guard your mail from theft. Deposit outgoing mail in post office collection boxes or at your local post office. Promptly remove mail from your mailbox after it has been delivered.

❖ Put passwords on your credit card, bank and phone accounts. Avoid using easily available information like your mother's maiden name, your birth date, the last four digits of your SSN or your phone number, or a series of consecutive numbers.

❖ Limit the identification information and the number of cards you carry to what you'll actually need.

❖ Do not give out personal information on the phone, through the mail or over the Internet unless you have initiated the contact or know whom you're dealing with. Identity thieves may pose as representatives of banks, Internet service providers and even government agencies to get you to reveal your SSN, mother's maiden name, financial account numbers and other identifying information. Legitimate organizations with which you do business have the information they need and will not ask you for it.

❖ Keep items with personal information in a safe place. To thwart an identity thief who may pick through your trash to take your personal information, tear or shred your charge receipts, copies of credit applications, insurance forms, bank checks and statements that you are discarding, expired charge cards and credit offers you get in the mail.

❖ Be cautious about where you leave personal information in your home, especially if you have roommates, employ outside help or are having service work done in your home.

❖ Find out who has access to your personal information at work and verify that the records are kept in a secure location.

❖ Give your SSN only when absolutely necessary. Ask to use other types of identifiers when possible.

❖ Don't carry your SSN card; leave it in a secure place.

❖ Order a copy of your credit report from each of the three major credit reporting agencies every year. Make sure it is accurate and includes only those activities you've authorized. The law allows credit bureaus to charge you up to $8.50 for a copy of your credit report.

Your credit report contains information on where you work and live, the credit accounts that have been opened in your name, how you pay your bills and whether you've been sued, arrested or filed for bankruptcy. Checking your report on a regular basis can help you catch mistakes and fraud before they ruin your personal finances.

Chapter Four

Six Action Steps
You Must Immediately Take If
Your Identity Is Stolen

Sometimes an identity thief can strike even if you've been very careful about keeping your personal information to yourself. If you suspect that your personal information has been hijacked and misappropriated to commit fraud or theft, take action immediately, and keep a record of your conversations and correspondence. Exactly which steps you should take to protect yourself depends on your circumstances and how your identity has been misused. However, should you unfortunately become an identity theft victim, do these six things immediately to stop a thief's further use of your identity:

1. File a report with your local police or the police where the identity theft took place. Make sure to get a copy of the report in case your bank, credit card company, or others need proof of the crime later on.

   Note: Many police departments are hesitant to write a report on this type of crime. First off, they may tell you that you are not the victim, because the credit grantor actually suffered the financial loss and is the real victim in their viewpoint.

The police frequently want the report to come from the creditor who many times will not cooperate because it is not cost effective from them to spend the time and energy to help the police. They may have already lost hundreds of thousands of dollars. Thus, to them, this fraud loss is perceived as a cost of doing business. While this is not fair to you as the victim, in many places that is the situation.

You must insist that the police take the report, even if the creditor won't prosecute. Speak to the head of the fraud unit or white-collar crime unit.

If accounts in your name were opened all over the nation, you may be able to get the Secret Service involved. The point is that you need a report to clean up the credit mess.

If you still have trouble, call and write to the Chief of Police. You may need to call the Mayor or the City Council. If you still get no result, call an attorney for further help.

2. Call all your credit card issuers to close or "flag" your accounts. Get replacement cards with new account numbers. Put passwords (*not* your mother's maiden name) on any new accounts you open. **NOTE:** When closing your account, request that it be possessed as "account closed at cardholder's request." This is much better than "card lost or stolen," because when this statement is reported to the credit card bureaus, it can be interpreted as blaming you for the loss.

3. Notify the fraud departments of each of the following three credit bureaus and report that your identity has been stolen. Ask that a "fraud alert" be placed on your file and that no new credit is granted without your approval.

Credit Bureaus:

Equifax—www.equifax.com

> To order your report, call: 800-685-1111 or write:
> P.O. Box 740241, Atlanta, GA 30374-0241
> To report fraud, call: 800-525-6285 and write:
> P.O. Box 740241, Atlanta, GA 30374-0241

Experian—www.experian.com

> To order your report, call: 888-EXPERIAN (397-3742) or write:
> P.O. Box 949, Allen TX 75013-0949
> To report fraud, call: 888-EXPERIAN (397-3742) and write:
> P.O. Box 949, Allen TX 75013-0949

Trans Union—www.tuc.com

> To order your report, call: 800-916-8800 or write:
> 760 Sproul Road, P.O. Box 390, Springfield, PA 19064-0390
> To report fraud, call: 800-680-7289 and write:
>   Fraud Victim Assistance Division
>   P.O. Box 6790
>   Fullerton, CA 92634

4. Contact your bank(s) and cancel your checking and savings accounts and obtain new account numbers. Ask the bank to issue you a secret password (again, not your mother's maiden name) that must be used in all transactions. Finally, put stop payments on any outstanding checks you are aware of.

   Note: If you have reason to believe that an identity thief has tampered with your bank accounts, checks or ATM card, close the accounts immediately. When you open new accounts, insist on password-only access to minimize the chance that an identity thief can violate the accounts.

5. In addition, if your checks have been stolen or misused, stop payment. Also contact the major check verification companies to request that they notify retailers using their databases not to accept these checks, or ask your bank to notify the check verification service with which it does business. The following check verification companies accept reports of check fraud directly from consumers:

CheckRite:	1-800-766-2748
Cross Check:	1-707-586-0551
Equifax:	1-800-437-5120
SCAN:	1-800-262-7771
International Check Services:	1-800-631-9656
National Processing Company:	1-800-526-5380
Telecheck:	1-800-710-9898

6. **Stolen mail.** If an identity thief has stolen your mail to get new credit cards, bank and credit card statements, pre-screened credit offers or tax information, or if an identity thief has falsified change-of-address forms, that's a crime. Report it to your local postal inspector. Contact your local post office for the phone number for the nearest postal inspection service office or check the Postal Service web site at
www.usps.gov/websites/depart/inspect
Will I Have To Apply For A New Social Number?

Perhaps, but first, a few basic facts are important. In 1935, the Social Security Number was established for benefit and tax purposes. In fact, during the first few decades that Social Security Numbers were issued, they carried the warning: "not to be used for identification."

Unfortunately, today, everyone wants your Social Security Number. Schools, banks, insurance companies and, even the military wants it. Why? Because it is an easy way for individuals and the government to identity and keep track of you. It is the one number you are apparently stuck with your whole life.

Social Security does not perform a background check to confirm if the information is valid. The following chart illustrates the purpose of the digital sequence that the Social Security Administration uses when issuing its numbers :

001–003	NEW HAMPSHIRE
004–007	MAINE
008–009	VERMONT
010–034	MASSACHUSETTS
035–039	RHODE ISLAND
040–049	CONNECTICUT
050–134	NEW YORK
135–158	NEW JERSEY
159–211	PENNSYLVANIA
212–220	MARYLAND
221–231	VIRGINIA
232–236	W. VIRGINIA
237–246	N. CAROLINA
247–251	S. CAROLINA
252–260	GEORGIA
261–267	FLORIDA
268–302	OHIO
303–317	INDIANA
318–361	ILLINOIS
362–386	MICHIGAN
387–399	WISCONSIN

400–407	KENTUCKY
408–415	TENNESSEE
416–424	ALABAMA
429–432	ARKANSAS
433–439	LOUISIANA
440–448	OKLAHOMA
449–467	TEXAS
478–485	MINNESOTA
475–485	IOWA
486–500	MISSOURI
501–502	N. DAKOTA
503–504	S. DAKOTA
405–508	NEBRASKA
509–515	KANSAS
516–517	MONTANA
518–519	IDAHO
520	WYOMING
521–524	COLORADO
525 & 585	NEW MEXICO
526–527	ARIZONA
528–529	UTAH
530	NEVADA
531–539	WASHINGTON
540–544	OREGON
545–573	CALIFORNIA
574	ALASKA
575–576	HAWAII
577–579	DISTRICT OF COLUMBIA
425–428 &587	MISSISSIPPI
580	VI VIRGIN ISLANDS
581–584	PR PUERTO RICO
585	NEW MEXICO

586	PI PACIFIC ISLANDS
587–588	MISSOURI
589–595	FLORIDA

Some sources have claimed that numbers above 900 were used when some state programs were converted to federal control, but current SSA documents claim no numbers above 799 have ever been used.

As of Feb 10, 1999 the most recent area numbers to have been assigned include 650-658, 667-675, and 680. This list is from the SSA's web site, which shows the highest group number assigned for each area.

The first three digits correspond to the state in which the card is applied for. These are the key digits. These "area numbers" are assigned to geographical locations. They were first assigned the same way that zip codes were later assigned. Area numbers assigned prior to 1972 are an indication of the SSA office, which originally issued the SSN. Since 1972 the area number in SSNs corresponds to the residence address given by the applicant on the application for the SSN.

Next, but less important, is the middle set of two digits ("group numbers.") This is not related to geography, but rather to the order in which SSN are issued for a specific area. It tells the approximate year of issue. An odd number, between 05 and 09, was probably issued before the late 1930's, and an even number from 10 on up was probably issued after that. Previously unused two-digit sequences of even numbers, between 02 and 08 began to be circulated more than 20 years ago.. In 1965, the system was changed so assignments continued with the low even numbers and the high odd numbers. So, group number for each area number are assigned in the following order:

1. Odd numbers, 01 to 09
2. Even numbers, 10 to 98
3. Even numbers, 02 to 08
4. Odd numbers, 11 to 99

The last set of four digits *(serial numbers)* is usually assigned in chronological order within each area and group number as the applications are processed. Serial number "000" is never used. Before 1965, when number assignment was transferred from filed offices to the central office, serial numbers may have been assigned in a weird order. (Some sources claim that 2000 and 7000 series numbers were assigned out of order. That no longer seems to be the case.) Currently, the serial numbers are assigned in strictly increasing order with each area and group combination.

Under certain circumstances, SSA may issue you a new SSN at your request if, after trying to resolve the problems brought on by identity theft, you continue to experience problems. Be very careful here. A new SSN may not resolve your identity theft problems, and may actually create new problems. For example, a new SSN does not necessarily ensure a new credit record because credit bureaus may combine the credit records from your old SSN with those from your new SSN. Even when the old credit information is not associated with your new SSN, the absence of any credit history under your new SSN may make it more difficult for you to get credit. And finally, there's no guarantee that an identity thief wouldn't also misuse a new SSN.

Notify the Social Security Administration's Office of the Inspector General if your Social Security number has been fraudulently used. To do this, call 1-800-269-0271, or write them at PO Box 17768, Baltimore, MD 21235. Have it changed if it has become linked with bad checks and credit.

Other Steps You Can Take

Although there's no question that identity thieves can ravage your personal finances, there are still some additional things you can do to take control of the situation. For example:

❖ **Investments.** If you believe that an identity thief has tampered with your securities investments or a brokerage account, immediately report it to your broker or account manager and to the Securities and Exchange Commission.

❖ **Phone service.** If an identity thief has established new phone service in your name; is making unauthorized calls that seem to come from and are billed to your cellular phone; or is using your calling card and PIN, contact your service provider immediately to cancel the account and/or calling card. Open new accounts and choose new PINs.

If you are having trouble getting fraudulent phone charges removed from your account, contact your state Public Utility Commission for local service providers or the Federal Communications Commission for long-distance service providers and cellular providers at **www.fcc.gov/ccb/enforce/complaints.html** or 1-888-CALL-FCC.

❖ **Employment.** If you believe someone is using your SSN to apply for a job or to work, that's a crime. Report it to the SSA's Fraud Hotline at 1-800-269-0271. Also call SSA at 1-800-772-1213 to verify the accuracy of the earnings reported on your SSN, and to request a copy of your Social Security Statement.

❖ **Bankruptcy.** If you believe someone has filed for bankruptcy using your name, write to the U.S. Trustee in the Region where the bankruptcy was filed. A listing of the U.S. Trustee Program's Regions can be found at **www.usdoj.gov/ust**, or look in the Blue Pages of your phone book under U.S. Government— Bankruptcy Administration.

Your letter should describe the situation and provide proof of your identity. The U.S. Trustee, if appropriate, will make a referral to criminal law enforcement authorities if you provide appropriate documentation to substantiate your claim. You also may want to file a complaint with the U.S. Attorney and/or the FBI in the city where the bankruptcy was filed.

❖ **Criminal records/arrests.** In rare instances, an identity thief may create a criminal record under your name. For example, your impostor may give your name when being arrested. If this happens to you, you may need to hire an attorney to help resolve the problem. The procedures for clearing your name vary by jurisdiction.

Chapter Five

Federal and State Laws That Deal With The Identity Theft Problem

Crime expands according to our willingness to put up with it.

—Barry Farber, 1947–

Federal Laws

The Federal government and numerous states have passed laws that address the problem of identity theft.

In October 1998, Congress passed The Identity Theft and Assumption Deterrence Act, (Identity Theft Act) to address the problem of identity theft. Specifically, the Act amended 18 U.S.C. §1028 to make it a federal crime when anyone:

> "knowingly transfers or uses, without lawful authority, a means of identification of another person with the intent to commit, or to aid or abet, any unlawful activity that constitutes a violation of federal law, or that constitutes a felony under any applicable state or local law."

Violations of the Act are investigated by federal law enforcement agencies, including the U.S. Secret Service, the FBI, the U.S. Postal Inspection Service and SSA's Office of the Inspector General. The U.S. Department of Justice prosecutes Federal identity theft cases.

Note that under the Act, a name or SSN is considered a "means of identification." So is a credit card number, cellular telephone electronic serial number or any other piece of information that may be used alone or in conjunction with other information to identify a specific individual.

The following are states that have passed identity theft laws. This list is subject to change since other states may be considering such legislation.

Arizona—Ariz. Rev. Stat. § 13-2708

In 1996, Arizona passed legislation adding section 2708 to title 13, Arizona Revised Statutes. Under this new section:

> a person commits identity fraud by knowingly taking the name, birth date or social security number of another person, without the consent of that other person, with the intent to obtain or use the other person's identity for any unlawful purpose or to cause financial loss to a person.

Further, under Arizona's statutes taking the identity of another person is a class 5 felony, punishable with imprisonment of 1-1/2 years, plus a fine of not more than $150,000.

According to an Arizona official, from the time of the 1996 enactment of the state's law to February 1998, the police had forwarded 142 investigative cases to county prosecutors, who had subsequently filed 89 court cases.

Arkansas Ark. Code Ann. § 5-37-227

§ 5-37-227. Financial identity fraud.

(a) (1)   A person commits financial identity fraud if, with the intent to unlawfully appropriate financial resources of another person to his or her own use or to the use of a third party, and without the authorization of that person, he or she:

      (A)   Obtains or records identifying information that would assist in accessing the financial resources of the other person; or

      (B)   Accesses or attempts to access the financial resources of the other person through the use of the identifying information, as defined in subdivision (a)(2) of this section.

  (2)   "Identifying information", as used in this section, includes, but is not limited to:

      (A)   Social security numbers;

      (B)   Driver's license numbers;

      (C)   Checking account numbers;

      (D)   Savings account numbers;

      (E)   Credit card numbers;

      (F)   Debit card numbers;

      (G)   Personal identification numbers;

      (H)   Electronic identification numbers;

      (I)   Digital signatures; or

      (J)   Any other numbers or information that can be used to access a person's financial resources.

(b) The provisions of this section do not apply to any person who obtains another person's driver's license or other form of identification for the sole purpose of misrepresenting his or her age.

(c) Financial identity fraud is a Class D felony.

(d) (1)   A violation of this section shall constitute an unfair or deceptive act or practice as defined by the Deceptive Trade Practices Act, § *4-88-101* et seq.

      (2)   All remedies, penalties, and authority granted to the Attorney General or other persons under the Deceptive Trade Practices Act, § *4-88-101* et seq., shall be available to the Attorney General or other persons for the enforcement of this section.

History. Acts 1999, No. 568, § 1; 1999, No. 1578, § 1.

California Cal. Penal Code § 530.5

In 1997, California added section 530.5 to the California Penal Code. Section 530.5, which came effective January 1, 1998, makes it a public offense to:

> (1) willfully obtains personal identifying information of another person without the authorization of that person and (2) use that information for any unlawful purpose, including to obtain, or attempt to obtain, credit, goods, services, or medical information in the name of the other person without the consent of that person. Under this law, "personal identifying information" is defined as the name, address, telephone number, driver's license number, SSN, place of employment, employee identification number, mother's maiden name, demand deposit account number, savings account number, or credit-card number of an individual.

Conviction under section 530.5 is punishable by imprisonment in a county jail not to exceed one year, a fine not to exceed one thousand dollars ($1,000), or both.

Connecticut *1999 Conn. Acts 99-99*

An Act Concerning Identity Theft.

> (NEW)   (a)   A person is guilty of identity theft when such person intentionally obtains personal identifying information of another person without the authorization of such other person and uses that information for any unlawful purpose including, but not limited to, obtaining, or attempting to obtain, credit, goods, services or medical information in the name of such other person without the

consent of such other person. As used in this section, "personal identifying information" means a motor vehicle operator's license number, Social Security number, employee identification number, mother's maiden name, demand deposit number, savings account number or credit card number.

(b)   Identity theft is a class D felony.

Georgia *Ga. Code Ann. §§ 121-127* (10/15/99)

16-9-121.

A person commits the offense of financial identity fraud when without the authorization or permission of another person and with the intent unlawfully to appropriate financial resources of that other person to his or her own use or to the use of a third party he or she:

(1) Obtains or records identifying information which would assistin accessing the financial resources of the other person; or

(2) Accesses or attempts to access the financial resources of theother person through the use of identifying information. Such identifying information shall include but not be limited to:

(A)   Social security numbers;

(B)   Driver's license numbers;

(C)   Checking account numbers;

(D)   Savings account numbers;

(E)   Credit card numbers;

(F)   Debit card numbers;

(G)   Personal identification numbers;

(H)   Electronic identification numbers;

(I)   Digital signatures; or

    (J)   Any other numbers or information which can be used to access a person's financial resources.

Idaho *Code § 28-3126*

MISAPPROPRIATION OF PERSONAL IDENTIFYING INFORMATION.

It is unlawful for any person to obtain or record personal identifying information of another person without the authorization of that person, with the intent that the information be used to obtain, or attempt to obtain, credit, money, goods or services in the name of the other person without the consent of that person.

Illinois *720 ILCS 5/16G*

ARTICLE 16G FINANCIAL IDENTITY THEFT AND ASSET FORFEITURE LAW

Sec. 16G-15. Financial identity theft.

(a) A person commits the offense of financial identity theft when he or she knowingly uses any personal identifying information or personal identification document of another person to fraudulently obtain credit, money, goods, services, or other property in the name of the other person.

(b) Knowledge shall be determined by an evaluation of all circumstances surrounding the use of the other person's identifying information or document.

(c) When a charge of financial identity theft of credit, money, goods, services, or other property exceeding a specified value is brought the value of the credit, money, goods, services, or other property is an element of the offense to be resolved by the trier of fact as either exceeding or not exceeding the specified value.

(d) Sentence.

(1) Financial identity theft of credit, money, goods, services, or other property not exceeding $300 in value is a Class A misdemeanor. A person who has been previously convicted of financial identity theft of less than $300 who is convicted of a second or subsequent offense of financial identity theft of less than $300 is guilty of a Class 4 felony.

(Source: P.A. 91-517, eff. 8-13-99.)

Iowa *Code § 715A.8)*

715A.8 Identity theft.

1. For purposes of this section, "identification information" means the name, address, date of birth, telephone number, driver's license number, nonoperator's identification number, social security number, place of employment, employee identification number, parent's legal surname prior to marriage, demand deposit account number, savings or checking account number, or credit card number of a person.

2. A person commits the offense of identity theft if the person with the intent to obtain a benefit fraudulently obtains identification information of another person and uses or attempts to use that information to obtain credit, property, or services without the authorization of that other person.

3. If the value of the credit, property, or services exceeds one thousand dollars, the person commits a class "D" felony. If the value of the credit, property, or services does not exceed one thousand dollars, the person commits an aggravated misdemeanor.

4. A violation of this section is an unlawful practice under section 714.16.

Maryland *Md. Ann. Code art. 27, § 231*

§ 231.

(a)   In this section, "personal identifying information" means the name, address, telephone number, driver's license number, social security number, place of employment, employee identification number, mother's maiden name, bank or other financial institution account number, date of birth, personal identification number, or credit card number of an individual.

(b)   A person may not knowingly, willfully, and with fraudulent intent obtain or aid another person in obtaining personal identifying information of an individual, without the consent of that individual, for the purpose of using that information or selling or transferring that information to obtain any benefit, credit, goods, services, or other item of value in the name of that individual.

(c)   A person may not knowingly and willfully assume the identity of another:

    (1)   With fraudulent intent to obtain any benefit, credit, goods, services, or other item of value;

    (2)   With fraudulent intent to avoid the payment of a debt or other legal obligation; or

    (3)   To avoid prosecution for a crime.

(d)   A person who violates this section is guilty of a misdemeanor and on conviction is subject to a fine not exceeding $5,000 or imprisonment in the penitentiary not exceeding 1 year or both.

(e)   In addition to the restitution provided under § 807 of this article, a court may order a person who pleads guilty or nolo contendere or is found guilty under this section to make restitution to the victim for reasonable costs incurred, including reasonable attorney's fees:

    (1)   For clearing the victim's credit history or credit rating; and

(2)   In connection with any civil or administrative proceeding to satisfy a debt, lien, judgment, or other obligation of the victim that arose as a result of the violation of this section.

(f) A sentence under this section may be imposed separate from and consecutive to or concurrent with a sentence for any offense based on the act or acts establishing the violation of this section.

Massachusetts *1998 Mass. Acts 397* (to be codified at Mass. Gen. Laws ch. 266, § 37E)

Chapter 397 of the Acts of 1998

AN ACT RELATIVE TO FALSE IMPERSONATION AND IDENTITY FRAUD.

SECTION 1. Chapter 266 of the General Laws is hereby amended by inserting after section 37D the

following section:—

Section 37E.

(a) For purposes of this section, the following words shall have the following meanings:-

"Harass", willfully and maliciously engage in an act directed at a specific person or persons, which act seriously alarms or annoys such person or persons and would cause a reasonable person to suffer substantial emotional distress.

"Personal identifying information", any name or number that may be used, alone or in conjunction with any other information, to assume the identity of an individual, including any name, address, telephone number, driver's license number, social security number, place of employment, employee identification number, mother's maiden name, demand deposit account number, savings account number, credit card number or computer password identification.

"Pose", to falsely represent oneself, directly or indirectly, as another person or persons.

"Victim", any person who has suffered financial loss or any entity that provided money, credit, goods, services or anything of value and has suffered financial loss as a direct result of the commission or attempted commission of a violation of this section.

(b) Whoever, with intent to defraud, poses as another person without the express authorization of that person and uses such person's personal identifying information to obtain or to attempt to obtain money, credit, goods, services, anything of value, any identification card or other evidence of such person's identity, or to harass another shall be guilty of identity fraud and shall be punished by a fine of not more than $5,000 or imprisonment in a house of correction for not more than two and one-half years, or by both such fine and imprisonment.

(c) Whoever, with intent to defraud, obtains personal identifying information about another person without the express authorization of such person, with the intent to pose as such person or who obtains personal identifying information about a person without the express authorization of such person in order to assist another to pose as such person in order to obtain money, credit, goods, services, anything of value, any identification card or other evidence of such person's identity, or to harass another shall be guilty of the crime of identity fraud and shall be punished by a fine of not more than $5,000 or imprisonment in a house of correction for not more than two and one-half years, or by both such fine and imprisonment.

(d) A person found guilty of violating any provisions of this section shall, in addition to any other punishment, be ordered to make restitution for financial loss sustained by a victim as a result of such violation. Financial loss may include any costs incurred by such victim in correcting the credit history of such victim or any costs incurred in connection with any civil or administrative proceeding to satisfy any debt or other obligation of such victim, including lost wages and attorney's fees.

SECTION 2. Chapter 268 of the General Laws is hereby amended by inserting after section 34 the following section:-

Section 34A. Whoever knowingly and willfully furnishes a false name or Social Security number to a law enforcement officer or law enforcement official following an arrest shall be punished by a fine of not more than $1,000 or by imprisonment in a house of correction for not more than one year or by both such fine and imprisonment. Such sentence shall run from and after any sentence imposed as a result of the underlying offense. The court may order that restitution be paid to persons whose identity has been assumed and who have suffered monetary losses as a result of a violation of this section.

Approved December 3, 1998.

Missouri *Mo. Rev. Stat. § 570.223*

Identity theft—penalty—restitution.

570.223. 1. A person commits the crime of identity theft if he knowingly and with the intent to deceive or defraud obtains, possesses, transfers, uses, or attempts to obtain, transfer or use, one or more means of identification not lawfully issued for his use.

2. Identity theft is punishable by up to six months in jail for the first offense; up to one year in jail for the second offense; and one to five years imprisonment for the third or subsequent offense.

In addition to the provisions of subsection 2 of this section, the court may order that the defendant make restitution to any victim of the offense. Restitution may include payment for any costs, including attorney fees, incurred by the victim:

(1)   In clearing the credit history or credit rating of the victim; and

(2)   In connection with any civil or administrative proceeding to satisfy any debt, lien, or other obligation of the victim arising from the actions of the defendant.

Oregon *House Bill 3057 (1999)*

SECTION 1.

(1) A person commits the crime of identity theft if the person, with the intent to defraud, obtains, possesses, transfers, creates, utters or converts to the person's own use the personal identification of another person.

(2) Identity theft is a Class C felony.

(3) It is an affirmative defense to violating subsection (1) of this section that the person charged with the offense: (a) Was under 21 years of age at the time of committing the offense and the person used the personal identification of another person solely for the purpose of purchasing alcohol; (b) Was under 18 years of age at the time of committing the offense and the person used the personal identification of another person solely for the purpose of purchasing tobacco products; or (c) Used the personal identification of another person solely for the purpose of misrepresenting the person's age to gain access to a: (A) Place the access to which is restricted based on age; or (B) Benefit based on age.

(4) As used in this section:

(a)   'Another person' means a real or imaginary person.

(b) 'Personal identification' includes, but is not limited to, any written document or electronic data that does, or purports to, provide information concerning: (A) A person's name, address or telephone number; (B) A person's driving privileges; (C) A person's Social Security number or tax identification number; (D) A person's citizenship status or alien identification number; (E) A person's employment status, employer or place of employment; (F) The identification number assigned to a person by a person's employer; (G) The maiden name of a person or a person's mother;

Tennessee *Tenn. Code Ann. § 39-14-150*

39-14-150. Identity theft.

(a) A person commits identity theft who knowingly transfers or uses, without lawful authority, a means of identification of another person with the intent to commit, or otherwise promote, carry on, or facilitate any unlawful activity.

(b) As used in this section, "means of identification" means any name or number that may be used, alone or in conjunction with any other information, to identify a specific individual, including:

 (1) Name, social security number, date of birth, official state or government issued driver license or identification number, alien registration number, passport number, employer or taxpayer identification number;

 (2) Unique biometric data, such as fingerprint, voice print, retina or iris image, or other unique physical representation;

 (3) Unique electronic identification number, address, routing code or other personal identifying data which enables an individual to obtain merchandise or service or to otherwise financially cncumber the legitimate possessor of the identifying data; or

(4)   Telecommunication identifying information or access device.

(c) A   violation   of   this   section   is   a   Class   D   felony.

[Acts 1999, ch. 57, § 1.]

Texas *Senate Bill 46 (1999)* (to be codified at Tex. Penal Code § 32.51)

SECTION 1. Subchapter D, Chapter 32, Penal Code, is amended by adding Section 32.51 to read as follows:

Sec. 32.51. FRAUDULENT USE OR POSSESSION OF IDENTIFYING INFORMATION.

(a) In this section:

   (1)   "Identifying information" means information that alone or in conjunction with other information identifies an individual, including an individual's:

   (A)   name, social security number, date of birth, and government-issued identification number;

   (B)   unique biometric data, including the individual's fingerprint, voice print, and retina or iris image;

   (C)   unique electronic identification number, address, and routing code; and

   (D)   telecommunication identifying information or access device.

   (2)   "Telecommunication access device" means a card, plate, code, account number, personal identification number, electronic serial number, mobile identification number, or other telecommunications service, equipment, or instrument identifier or means of account access that

alone or in conjunction with another telecommunication access device may be used to:

(A)   obtain money, goods, services, or other thing of value; or

(B)   initiate a transfer of funds other than a transfer originated solely by paper instrument.

(b)   A person commits an offense if the person obtains, possesses, transfers, or uses identifying information of another person without the other person's consent and with intent to harm or defraud another.

(c)   An offense under this section is a state jail felony.

(d)   If a court orders a defendant convicted of an offense under this section to make restitution to the victim of the offense, the court may order the defendant to reimburse the victim for lost income or other expenses, other than attorney's fees, incurred as a result of the offense.

(e)   If conduct that constitutes an offense under this section also constitutes an offense under any other law, the actor may be prosecuted under this section or the other law.

SECTION 2. This Act takes effect September 1, 1999.

SECTION 3. The importance of this legislation and the crowded condition of the calendars in both houses create an emergency and an imperative public necessity that the constitutional rule requiring bills to be read on three several days in each house be suspended, and this rule is hereby suspended.

Washington *Wash. Rev. Code § 9.35* (**RCW 9.35.020 Identity theft.** *(Effective January 1, 2000.)*

(1).   No person may knowingly use or knowingly transfer a means of identification of another person with the intent to commit, or to aid or abet, any unlawful activity harming or intending to harm the person whose identity is used, or for committing any felony.

(2). For purposes of this section, "means of identification" means any information or item that is not describing finances or credit but is personal to or identifiable with any individual or other person, including any current or former name of the person, telephone number, and electronic address or identifier of the individual or any member of his or her family, including the ancestor of such person; any information relating to a change in name, address, telephone number, or electronic address or identifier of the individual or his or her family; any social security, driver's license, or tax identification number of the individual or any member of his or her family; and other information which could be used to identify the person, including unique biometric data.

(3) Violation of this section is a class C felony.

(4) A person that [who] violates this section is liable for five hundred dollars or actual damages, including costs to repair the person's credit record, whichever is greater, and reasonable attorneys' fees. If the person violating this section is a business that repeatedly violates this section, that person also violates the Consumer Protection Act, *chapter 19.86 RCW.*

Chapter Six

Case Files: Those Busted for Stealing Identities

People always overdo the matter when they attempt deception.

—Charles Dudley Warner (1871)

The following cases all pertain to identity theft showing how the law handled those violating ID theft laws.

San Diego County Woman sentenced To Federal Prison for stealing Identity of University Professor

SAN DIEGO, CA, 1999—Theresa Marie Thompson-Snow, a Chula Vista woman who admitted using a stolen social security number to obtain thousands of dollars in credit and then filing for bankruptcy in the name of her victim was sentenced to 16 months in federal prison.

Thompson-Snow pleaded guilty to three counts of false representation of a social security number and one count of bankruptcy fraud. By pleading guilty, Thompson-Snow admitted that she assumed the identity of another woman with a similar name in order to obtain loans that Thompson-Snow was not qualified to receive. The defendant, who was a licensed notary public at the time had been employed as a paralegal, defaulted on the loans. In January 1997, Thompson-Snow sought to avoid the consequences of the defaults by fraudulently filing for bankruptcy.

The FBI began investigating the case after the victim, Theresa Mae Thompson, an English professor at Valdosta State University in South Georgia, contacted it. Professor Thompson had graduated from a college in Arizona that the defendant also briefly attended, and both women had received student loans that were administered through the same company. Due to a computer mix-up, documents belonging to Professor Thompson, which included her social security number—were sent to the defendant in 1995.

Shortly thereafter, Professor Thompson began receiving telephone calls from companies that she had never heard of claiming she owed them large sums of money.

During the sentencing hearing in Los Angeles, Assistant United States Attorney Ranee Katzenstein argued that Thompson-Snow had continued to engage in fraudulent conduct while awaiting sentencing. After the sentencing, the Judge immediately remanded the defendant into custody, finding that Thompson-Snow had not been "forthcoming" with the court. Judge Marshall also said she "could not find that she [Thompson-Snow] would not continue to be involved with illegal activity."

In addition to the prison term, the Judge imposed restitution in the amount of $13,928 and ordered the defendant to pay a $5000 criminal fine.

Former Insurance Company Worker Pleads Guilty to identity Theft In Scheme to Defraud Banks and Policyholders

LOS ANGELES, CA, October, 1999—Anthony Jerome Johnson, an Inglewood, California man pleaded guilty to federal charges for obtaining private bank account information about an insurance company's policyholders and using that information to deposit three-quarters of a million dollars in counterfeit checks into a bank account he established.

Johnson's case represented the first time a defendant had been convicted of theft of identity, 18 U.S.C. § 1028(a)(7), in the Central District of California. This new federal law was enacted when the

United States Congress passed the *Identity Theft and Assumption Deterrence Act of 1998.*

In a plea agreement filed in United States District Court in Los Angeles, Johnson admitted that he was responsible for counterfeiting approximately 4,300 bank drafts that he deposited with MBNA America in Delaware to obtain approximately $764,000 from the bank accounts of Aurora policyholders.

Johnson directed a printing company in Texas to generate the bank drafts, which were made payable to SSS Consultants, a company that Johnson controlled.

As part of the scheme, Johnson took the identity of a Southern California man named Donald Lightfoot in an attempt to complete the scheme to obtain the $764,000.

Johnson was arrested by special agents with the Federal Bureau of Investigation in August 1999 less than one week after Aurora learned about the alleged fraud scheme and reported it to federal authorities. Aurora fully cooperated with the federal investigation.

Through a temporary employment agency, Johnson obtained a job at Aurora in late March and worked at the company until July 1. In August, officials at Aurora began receiving complaints from policyholders who typically pay their premiums through electronic fund transfers that unauthorized withdrawals had been made from their accounts. Subsequent investigation revealed that the 4,300 checks—totaling approximately $746,000—had just been deposited into an account in the name of SSS Consultants, Inc. at MBNA.

Johnson, disguised as "Donald Lightfoot," opened two other bank accounts, telling representatives at the other two banks that he was planning to make large wire transfers to the accounts. However, Johnson was not successful in making the wire transfers. All of the money deposited into the MBNA account had been recovered.

Bank fraud carries a potential penalty of 30 years in federal prison; wire fraud carries a sentence of up to 30 years in federal prison; and identity theft carries a maximum possible penalty of three years imprisonment. Therefore, the maximum possible that Johnson faced was 123 years in federal prison, as well as fines that could total $4.25 million.

Nine Charged In Identity Fraud Scheme: 49 aliases included phony businesses, false and Stolen Names

COLUMBUS, OHIO, July, 1999—A federal grand jury charged nine people with setting up a complex scheme involving the creation of fake identities and phony businesses. They also were using multiple addresses and counterfeit checks and money orders to defraud banks and businesses.

The grand jury alleged that the conspiracy dated back to 1994. The defendants were accused of creating and using false identities to open accounts at American Express Travel Related Services Company, Inc., and at several financial institutions. The defendants allegedly used individual and shared addresses and telephone numbers to open and maintain accounts at several financial institutions.

The indictment stated that they deposited worthless, counterfeit and stolen money, securities and monetary instruments at several financial institutions, then caused money which had been credited to the accounts to be withdrawn before the financial institutions learned that the items deposited were worthless, counterfeit and stolen. They were also charged with conducting financial transactions individually and among themselves in order to conceal and disguise the proceeds of bank fraud.

Specific charges in the 151-count indictment included identity fraud, money laundering conspiracy, money laundering, counterfeiting, using fraudulent access devices, bank fraud, and Social Security account number fraud. Money laundering conspiracy and bank frauds have maximum penalties of 30 years imprisonment and a fine of up to $1 million. The maximum penalty for money laundering is 20 years imprisonment. Identity fraud has a 15-year maximum penalty.

Fraudulent access devices and counterfeiting have ten-year maximum penalties, and Social Security number fraud has a maximum five-year penalty.

Note: Of course, it is important to know that an indictment is merely an accusation. Defendants are always presumed innocent until and unless proven guilty.

Defendant Sentenced for Violating Federal "Identity Theft" statute after stealing Computers from Wisconsin Supreme Court

MADISON, WISCONSIN, September, 1999—Waverly C. Burns, was sentenced to 21 months imprisonment and three years supervised release before United States District Court Judge Barbara B. Crabb. Burns had pleaded guilty to identity theft on July 29, 1999. Burns had fraudulently used the identity of James W. Clark to obtain employment with Clean Power in Madison, then using that employment to commit a burglary.

The Facts:

Through his job at Clean Power, Burns gained access to the offices of the Wisconsin Supreme Court in the Tenney Building at 110 East Main Street, Madison. On January 3, 1999, wearing a name badge bearing the name "James Clark," Burns entered the Tenney Building and took six computer monitors owned by the State of Wisconsin. The monitors were recovered almost immediately following the burglary, after Burns abandoned the vehicle that he was driving.

Burns was ordered to pay restitution as follows: Bureau of Justice Information Services—$52,040; Wisconsin Supreme Court—$3,679.63; Woodman's Food Store—$295.02, and Social Security Administration—$6,834.78.

Defendant Sentenced For Using Others' Identities To Collect Social Security Benefits

SANTA CLARA, CA—On September 27, 1999, Alexander Winfield, also known as Don Lafon, was sentenced to a term of twenty-three (23) months imprisonment following his conviction for stealing $262,279.45 in Social Security benefits, violating Title 18 USC Sec. 641. The sentence also called for Winfield to pay full restitution to the Social Security Administration in the amount of $262,279.45, as well as serving three years supervised release.

The Facts:

From 1974 to 1998, Winfield had used four identities and social security numbers, including the identity and social security number of his deceased stepfather, to get SSI and SSDI benefits totaling $262,279.45. Winfield had also provided false statements to the Administration in an effort to hide other sources of income such as workers compensation and private disability benefits.

Man Arrested in Woodbridge Township in Identity Fraud Scheme

TRENTON, NJ, December, 1999—Division of Criminal Justice investigators and Woodbridge Township Police arrested Danny Moore, no known address. The charges were that he engaged in an identity theft scheme in which he obtained personal information about an individual, created fraudulent identification using his own photograph with the stolen identity and then used the stolen identity to purchase goods, cash checks, and engage in other bank transactions. Moore was alleged to have even incurred traffic violations under the stolen identity.

The authorities became aware of the problem when one of the individuals, whose identity had been stolen, received bills for goods he never purchased and notices of failure to appear for hearings on traffic summonses he never received. He then reported the matter to law enforcement authorities.

Moore was charged with Wrongful Impersonation (Identity Theft), Theft by Deception, Passing Bad Checks and Credit Card Fraud. The Wrongful Impersonation statute was amended by the Legislature in 1995 to enhance the penalties for such crimes.

West Palm Beach Woman Guilty of ID Fraud

WEST PALM BEACH, FLORIDA—On August 18, 1999, TERKESHA LANE, 21, from West Palm Beach, pled guilty to identity fraud. Lane was charged with using the identity of another person to commit bank fraud, credit card fraud, and grand theft. Lane worked at the same company as the victim, and obtained a fraudulent Florida driver's license in the name of the victim. She then used the driver's license to withdraw over $13,000 from the victim's bank account at First Union Bank. Lane also obtained five department store credit cards in the victim's name, then charged approximately $4000 on those cards.

FBI Arrest Two Women Charged With Bank Fraud

SAN DIEGO, CA, October, 1999—FBI Agents took Cardie Mae Kelly Gold and Leilani Denise Fails into custody without incident. Gold, born September 24, 1945, was arrested at her residence: 8124 Paradise Valley Court in Spring Valley. Simultaneously, Fails, born September 16, 1962, was arrested at her residence: 3518 Sandrock Road in San Diego.

Both Gold and Fails were arrested based on an indictment filed in U. S. District Court in San Diego on October 12, 1999. Fails allegedly used a fraudulent identification to open a Bank of America account. It is believed she made deposits and withdrawals of stolen checks over a two-week period in October of 1996, and ultimately cashed out in excess of $77,000.

The indictment also alleged that Gold, who was employed as a Customer Service Manager at the Barrio Logan Branch of the Bank of America, assisted Fails in these endeavors.

Fails is alleged to have stolen an actual Bank of America customer's identity and overlapped the information onto a stolen Union Bank customer's checks to further the scheme.

Attorney General Announces Sentencing in Fraud and Identity Theft Case

PHOENIX, AZ, February, 1999—Attorney General Janet Napolitano announced the sentencing of a woman who stole women's identities and defrauded banks and other businesses in Tucson. Initially arrested under the name of one of the victims in the case, the suspect only later admitted her real name, Cynthia Wood. Wood was arrested in October, months after the victim's identification was stolen from Oakland, California. Wood was sentenced to seven years in prison and was ordered to pay nearly $33,000 in restitution.

Wood had also assumed the identity of 12 other women. While the victims were having lunch at restaurants around Tucson, Wood would remove drivers' licenses, credit cards and other valuables. She would then paste her photo over the victims' license photos and present the license and victims' credit cards or checks to banks. In some instances, Wood worked quickly, getting cash advances and cashing checks, often before victims finished their lunches.

Wood was the second person convicted for identity theft in Tucson by the Attorney General's Office in 1999. Earlier, Rhonda Jean Raymond was sentenced to six years in prison and ordered to pay $15,000 in restitution.

Crackdown Hits 43 Phony Credit Firms Selling New Credit Profiles

February, 1999—In a massive crackdown on operators who turn credit-challenged Consumers into lawbreakers, 17 law enforcement agencies filed 43 law enforcement actions against defendants who claim to help consumers get new credit histories through new identification numbers—a practice known as "file segregation."

The firms in question advertised their services in newspapers, magazines and on Internet sites, using such claims as "ERASE BAD CREDIT", "ANYONE CAN HAVE A NEW CREDIT FILE INSTANTLY OVERNIGHT," and "START ALL OVER AGAIN WITH BRAND NEW CREDIT."

Many of the ads claim that, "It's 100% LEGAL…" or "It's not only legal, it's your right." For fees ranging from $29.95 to $200.00, the companies offer to sell consumers the instructions they need to apply to the Internal Revenue Service for employer or taxpayer identification numbers.

Consumers were typically counseled to use the new ID number in place of their social security number when applying for credit. They frequently were given advice how to develop whole new credit profiles by doing such things as getting new driver's licenses using the new I.D. number and advised about places that would give consumers "starter credit" using the new number. Using a false social security number—such as a taxpayer I.D. number—to apply for credit violates federal law and has been prosecuted vigorously by the IRS and U.S. Attorneys.

In addition, 21 cases were filed by the Attorneys General of Arizona, California, Connecticut, Delaware, Illinois, Kentucky, Minnesota, Missouri, Nevada, North Carolina, Ohio, Oklahoma, Oregon and Pennsylvania.

The bottom line is this: it takes time to rebuild a good credit reputation. There is no legal way for you to change your credit identification to hide adverse information that is correct and current!

Chapter Seven

Solutions You Can Use In Resolving Credit Problems Resulting From Having Your Identity Stolen

---

Experience is not what happens to a man. It is what a man does with what happens to him.

Aldous Leonard Huxley, 1894–1963

Resolving credit problems resulting from identity theft can be time-consuming and frustrating. The good news is that there are federal laws that establish procedures for correcting credit report errors and billing errors, and for stopping debt collectors from contacting you about debts you don't owe.

Here is a brief summary of your rights, and what to do to clear up credit problems that result from identity theft.

Credit Reports

The Fair Credit Reporting Act (FCRA) establishes procedures for correcting mistakes on your credit record and requires that your record be made available only for certain legitimate business needs.

Under the FCRA, both the credit bureau and the organization that provided the information to the credit bureau (the "information provider"), such as a bank or credit card company are responsible for correcting inaccurate or incomplete information in your report. To protect your rights under the law, contact both the credit bureau and the information provider.

First, call the credit bureau and follow up in writing. Tell them what information you believe is inaccurate. Include copies (NOT originals) of documents that support your position. In addition to providing your complete name and address, your letter should clearly identify each item in your report that you dispute, give the facts and explain why you dispute the information, and request deletion or correction. You may want to enclose a copy of your report with circles around the items in question. Send your letter by certified mail, and request a return receipt so you can document what the credit bureau received and when. Keep copies of your dispute letter and enclosures.

Credit bureaus must investigate the items in question — usually within 30 days—unless they consider your dispute frivolous. They also must forward all relevant data you provide about the dispute to the information provider. After the information provider receives notice of a dispute from the credit bureau, it must investigate, review all relevant information provided by the credit bureau and report the results to the credit bureau. If the information provider finds the disputed information to be inaccurate, it must notify all nationwide credit bureaus so they can correct this information in your file. Note that:

❖ Disputed information that cannot be verified must be deleted from your file.

❖ If your report contains erroneous information, the credit bureau must correct it.

❖ If an item is incomplete, the credit bureau must complete it. For example, if your file shows that you have been late making payments, but fails to show that you are no longer delinquent, the credit bureau must show that you're current.

❖ If your file shows an account that belongs to someone else, the credit bureau must delete it.

When the investigation is complete, the credit bureau must give you the written results and a free copy of your report if the dispute results in a change. If an item is changed or removed, the credit bureau cannot put the disputed information back in your file unless the information provider verifies its accuracy and completeness. Then, the credit bureau gives you a written notice that includes the name, address and phone number of the information provider.

If you request, the credit bureau must send notices of corrections to anyone who received your report in the past six months. Job applicants can have a corrected copy of their report sent to anyone who received a copy during the past two years for employment purposes. If an investigation does not resolve your dispute, ask the credit bureau to include your statement of the dispute in your file and in future reports.

Second, in addition to writing to the credit bureau, tell the creditor or other information provider *in writing* that you dispute an item. Again, include copies (NOT originals) of documents that support your position. Many information providers specify an address for disputes. If the information provider then reports the item to any credit bureau, it must include a notice of your dispute. In addition, if you are correct that is, if the disputed information is not accurate — the information provider may not use it again. If you have Internet access, you should also contact these two online consumer protection services:

TRUSTe
1180 Coleman Avenue, Suite 202
San Jose, CA 95110
(408) 342-1940; FAX: (408) 342-1950
Website: **www.truste.org**; E-mail: info@truste.org

TRUSTe is an independent, non-profit privacy organizations whose mission is to build users' trust and confidence on the Internet and, in doing so, accelerate growth of the Internet industry. The TRUSTe privacy program-based on a branded online seal, the TRUSTe "trustmark" -bridges the gap between users' concerns over privacy and Web sites' desire for self-regulated information disclosure standards.

> ePublicEye.com
> 427 W. Colorado
> Glendale,CA.91204
> Phone:818/547-0222
> Website: **www.epubliceye.com**; Email: wms@epubliceye.com

ePublicEye.com is an independent third party that allows consumers to rate e-business for reliability, privacy and customer satisfaction. Its interactive Open Customer Satisfaction Reporting system (OCSR) uses customer feedback to let consumers identify companies that are reliable and committed to customer satisfaction. ePublicEye.com is the first company to use consumer intelligence to empower both consumers and merchants.

Checking Your Credit on the Internet

Here are some places on the web where you can do a quick check of your credit:

1. The Credit Infocenter (**www.creditinfocenter.com**). This site teaches you how your credit is calculated, and how to actually read your credit report. There's also ways for improving your credit. You can even download free credit repair and dispute letters.
2. The Federal Trade Commission's *Back In The Black* (**www.ftc.gov/bcp/conline/edcams/repair/**). This site offers a reliable summary of what you can do to clean up your credit and avoid credit rip offs.

3. www.freecreditreport.com

   The Credit Basic area of this web site contains a wealth of information about credit, the credit reporting industry, and how you can take charge of your own personal credit. You can order a *free* copy of your online credit report from one of the three national credit bureaus. You can choose to either have your reports delivered online over the Internet or by U.S. mail. For more information contact them online at **www.freecreditreport.com** or **www.consumerinfo.com**. The mailing address is:

   ConsumerInfo.Com
   One City Blvd., Suite 401
   Orange, CA 92868
   1-888-888-8553; FAX: 1-714-978-0059;
   E-mail: visitor@consumerinfo.com

Credit Cards

The Fair Credit Billing Act establishes procedures for resolving billing errors on your credit card accounts. It also limits your liability for unauthorized credit card charges in most cases to $50 per card.

The Act's settlement procedures apply to disputes about "billing errors." This includes fraudulent charges on your accounts.

To take advantage of the law's consumer protections, you *must*:

❖ Write to the creditor at the address given for "billing inquiries," not the address for sending your payments. Include your name, address, account number and a description of the billing error, including the amount and date of the error.

❖ Send your letter so that it reaches the creditor within 60 days after the first bill containing the error was mailed to you. If an identity thief changed the address on your account and you never received the bill, your dispute letter still must reach the creditor within 60 days of when the creditor would have mailed the bill. This is why it's so important to keep track of your billing statements and immediately follow up when your bills don't arrive on time.

Send your letter by certified mail, and request a return receipt. This will be your proof of the date the creditor received the letter. Include copies (NOT originals) of sales slips or other documents that support your position. Keep a copy of your dispute letter.

The creditor must acknowledge your complaint in writing within 30 days after receiving it, unless the problem has been resolved. The creditor must resolve the dispute within two billing cycles (but not more than 90 days) after receiving your letter.

Debt Collectors

The Fair Debt Collection Practices Act prohibits debt collectors from using unfair or deceptive practices to collect overdue bills that a creditor has forwarded for collection.

You can stop a debt collector from contacting you by writing a letter to the collection agency telling them to stop. Once the debt collector receives your letter, the company may not contact you again with two exceptions: they can tell you there will be no further contact and they can tell you that the debt collector or the creditor intends to take some specific action.

A collector also may not contact you if, within 30 days after you receive the written notice, you send the collection agency a letter stating you do not owe the money. Although such a letter should stop the debt collector's calls, it will not necessarily get rid of the debt itself, which may still turn up on your credit report. In addition, a collector can renew collection activities if you are sent proof of the debt. So, along with your letter stating you don't owe the money, include copies of documents that support your position. If you're a victim of identity theft, including a copy (NOT original) of the police report you filed may be particularly useful.

ATM Cards, Debit Cards and Electronic Fund Transfers

The Electronic Fund Transfer Act provides consumer protections for transactions involving an ATM or debit card or other electronic way to debit or credit an account. It also limits your liability for unauthorized electronic fund transfers.

It's important to report lost or stolen ATM and debit cards immediately because the amount you can be held responsible for depends on *how quickly* you report the loss.

❖ If you report your ATM card lost or stolen within two business days of discovering the loss or theft, your losses are limited to $50.

❖ If you report your ATM card lost or stolen after the two business days, but within 60 days after a statement showing an unauthorized electronic fund transfer, you can be liable for up to $500 of what a thief withdraws.

❖ If you wait more than 60 days, you could lose *all* the money that was taken from your account after the end of the 60 days and before you report your card missing.

The best way to protect yourself in the event of an error or fraudulent transaction is to call the financial institution and follow up in writing—by certified letter, return receipt requested so you can prove when the institution received your letter. Keep a copy of the letter you send for your records.

After notification about an error on your statement, the institution generally has 10 business days to investigate. The financial institution must tell you the results of its investigation within three business days after completing it and must correct an error within one business day after determining that the error has occurred. If the institution needs more time, it may take up to 45 days to complete the investigation but only if the money in dispute is returned to your account and you are notified promptly of the credit. At the end of the investigation, if no error has been found, the institution may take the money back if it sends you a written explanation.

A Special Word About Lost or Stolen Checks

While no federal law limits your losses if someone steals your checks and forges your signature, state laws protect you. Most states hold the bank responsible for losses from a forged check. At the same time, however, most states require you to take reasonable care of your account. For example, You may be held responsible for the forgery if you fail to notify the bank in a timely manner that a check was lost or stolen. Contact your state banking or consumer protection agency for more information.

Note: VISA and MasterCard voluntarily have agreed to limit consumers' liability for unauthorized use of their debit cards in most instances to $50 per card, no matter how much time has elapsed since the discovery of the loss or theft of the card.

Conclusions

Once your identity has been stolen, it can pose a serious threat to your privacy and potentially can make your life a living hell. This book has provided a detailed overview of the major factors contributing to identity theft, as well as possible ways of preventing it, and failing that, dealing with it.

Identity theft must be handled in the following ways. First, applying fair, unbiased information practices, informing you what data is being collected; allowing you to opt out of the collection process; and giving you access to your own personal information. Second, as computers and networks make it easier to gather your personal information, hi-tech methods of protecting privacy will become increasingly important. Those groups that can insure the privacy and safety of their clients' financial and credit identities will gain a decisive competitive advantage over those failing to do so.

About the Author

Ron Patton is a certified handwriting expert. As President of Twintwo Communications, Inc., he has edited and published self-help books such as, *How To Get $500 From Telemarketers When They Won't Stop Calling You!*

Appendix A—Sample Letters, Forms & Checklists

Credit Report Request Form

Date:

To:

From:
Name, address
SS# or TIN/EIN#
Year of birth

To Whom It May Concern,

Please send me the following:
  []   My free annual copy of my credit file.
  []   I have enclosed a copy of a rejection notice indicating that I have been denied credit within the last 30 days. Please send me a free copy of my credit file.
  []   I am enclosing $, the required fee for a copy of my credit file. I am also including verification of current home address:
  []   a photocopy of my utility bill
  []   a copy of my driver license
  []   other proof of residence
Thank you,

(Your signature)

Sample Dispute Letter—Credit Bureau

Date
Your Name
Your Address
Your City, State, Zip Code

Complaint Department
Name of Credit Bureau
Address
City, State, Zip Code

Dear Sir or Madam:

I am writing to dispute the following information in my file. The items I dispute also are circled on the attached copy of the report I received. (Identify item(s) disputed by name of source, such as creditors or tax court, and identify type of item, such as credit account, judgment, etc.)

This item is (inaccurate or incomplete) because (describe what is inaccurate or incomplete and why). I am requesting that the item be deleted (or request another specific change) to correct the information.

Enclosed are copies of (use this sentence if applicable and describe any enclosed documentation, such as payment records, court documents) supporting my position.

Please investigate this (these) matter(s) and (delete or correct) the disputed item(s) as soon as possible.

Sincerely,

Your name

Enclosures: (List what you are enclosing.)

Sample Dispute Letter—Credit Card Issuers

Date
Your Name
Your Address
Your City, State, Zip Code
Your Account Number
Name of Creditor
Billing Inquiries
Address
City, State, Zip Code

Dear Sir or Madam:

I am writing to dispute a billing error in the amount of $_____on my account. The amount is inaccurate because (describe the problem). I am requesting that the error be corrected, that any finance and other charges related to the disputed amount be credited as well, and that I receive an accurate statement.

Enclosed are copies of (use this sentence to describe any enclosed information, such as sales slips, payment records) supporting my position. Please investigate this matter and correct the billing error as soon as possible.

Sincerely,
Your name

Enclosures: (List what you are enclosing.)

According to the Fair Credit Reporting Act you have the right to submit a 100 word or less statement to explain circumstances behind any negative reporting on your credit file. This can be for individual items or your credit file in general. Use this form letter for this purpose. Your consumer statement must be less than 100 words in length but otherwise can contain anything you desire.

Sample 100 Word Statement Letter

Date:

To: Put credit agency name and address here

From:
Name, address
SS# or TIN/EIN#
Year of birth
Phone number
Credit file #

To Whom it May Concern,

I would like to make the following consumer statement to be included in my credit file:

(Put your 100 word statement here)

Thank you,
(Your signature)

Sample Follow up Letter

Date:

To: (Put credit agency name and address here)

From:
Name, address
SS# or TIN/EIN#
Year of birth
Phone number
Credit file #

To Whom it May Concern,

Thirty days ago I sent you a letter requesting you to investigate item(s) on my credit file. I have enclosed a copy of that letter. I have not received any correspondence from you, and a reasonable time period has past that you were unable to verify the information or found it to be inaccurate. I now request that you remove the item(s) from my credit report and send me an updated report reflecting the corrections.

Thank you,

(Your signature)

U.S. Postal Inspection Service
Mail Fraud Questionnaire

Please be advised, information which you provide will be protected and only disclosed in accordance with the Privacy Act of 1974. A full disclosure statement can be found on the last page of this form.

CUSTOMER INFORMATION

Name :
Address :
City :
State :
ZIP Code :

Home telephone number:
Work telephone number:

Optional- Sentencing guidelines for certain crimes committed against those over the age of 55 allow for increased penalties. Can you be considered in this group? (check one) _____YES
_____NO

COMPLAINT AGAINST

Company/Individual Name:
Address :
City :
State :
ZIP Code :
Foreign Country :

Telephone number :
Internet Address :
Name of person you spoke with _____

Did you lose money? ____YES If yes, how much? $_____ ____NO

How did you first learn about the offer?

_____ US Mail
_____ Telephone
_____ Newspaper
_____ Magazine
_____ Radio
_____ TV
_____ Internet
_____ Other (describe) _____

When? ___/___/___

Do you still have the mailing envelope? YES___ NO___

advertisement? YES___ NO___

Internet message? YES___ NO___

Does the mailing envelope have a mailing permit number in the area where a stamp is normally placed? (Please copy the exact words)

_____

_____

How did you respond to the offer?

_____ US Mail

_____ Telephone
_____ Internet

Do you have any proof of mailing to the subject of your complaint?

_____ YES If yes, type and # _____
_____ NO

Any other uses of the US Mails? YES_____ NO_____

Invoices _____
Products _____
Correspondence _____
Cost of the Product or Service $_____
Amount paid to date $_____

How was payment made?

_____ Cash
_____ Check
_____ Money Order: _____USPS _____Other
_____ Electronic Transfer
_____ Debit Card
_____ Credit Card

Payment copies available? _____Yes _____No

Date of payment ___/___/___

Address payment mailed to, if different than the address of the subject of your complaint

_____

What was offered?

_____

_____

_____

_____

What was received for your money?

Nothing _____ Other _____

_____

_____

_____

_____

Do you still have it? YES_____ NO_____

How was it delivered?

_____ US Mail

_____ In person
_____ COD
_____ United Parcel Service (UPS)
_____ Federal Express (FedEx)
_____ Emery
_____ Puralator
_____ Airborne Express
_____ RPS
_____ Other(describe)_____

Do you have the mailing envelope or packaging? _____Yes _____No

Did it have a postage meter or permit number? _____

Have you contacted company / individual about your complaint?

_____YES Date_____
_____NO Why? _____Moved left no address
_____Unanswered telephone
_____Telephone disconnected
_____Unlisted telephone
_____Other (describe)_____

Did you request a refund? _____YES If yes, Date ___/___/___
_____NO

Did you receive a refund? _____YES If yes, Date ___/___/___
_____NO

Date of last contact with firm / individual ___/___/___

Additional Comments:_____

Please be advised, information which you provide will be protected and only disclosed in accordance with the Privacy Act of 1974. A full disclosure statement can be found on the last page of this form.

Please forward your completed Mail Fraud Questionnaire by US Mail to the address below which corresponds to the ZIP Code of the SUBJECT OF COMPLAINT. However, all chain letters regardless of ZIP Code, are handled by the Newark Inspection Service Support Group. Chain letters refer to letters which invite payment of small sums of money to 4 or 5 people and the distribution of the same letter with the new participant's name added, to several additional people. Chain letters are a form of lottery and as such are illegal to mail (or deliver in person or by computer, but mailing money to participate) in violation of Title 18, United States Code Section 1302, the Postal Lottery Statute.

Inspection Service Operations Support Group ALL CHAIN LETTERS.
ZIP Codes 003-079, 085-149

Fraud Complaint Supervisor ,
2 Gateway Center, Fl 9
Newark, NJ 07175-0001

Inspection Service Operations Support Group
ZIP Codes 080-084, 150-299, 37620-37625, 400-699, 800-999 (except 885)

Fraud Complaint Supervisor

222 S Riverside Plaza, Ste. 1250
Chicago, IL 60606-6100

Inspection Service Operations Support Group ALL FOREIGN
COMPLAINTS.
ZIP Codes 300-375, all 376 (except 37620-37625) 377-397, 700-799, 885

Fraud Complaint Supervisor
225 N Humphreys Blvd, Fl 4
Memphis, TN 38161-006

I am sure the actions of these debt collectors must be in violation of
various state consumer protections law statutes as well. Please send me

---

Complaint Letter To The State Attorney General's Office

Date: _____

Consumer Protection Division
State of _____ Attorney General's Office

_____

_____

Dear Sir or Madam:

I am being harassed by several debt collection agencies and request
that you immediately send to me all of the proper forms so that I may
file a complaint with your agency about violations of the following two
federal laws:
The Fair Debt collections Practices Act The Fair Credit Reporting Act

---

the necessary paperwork so that I may take action against these individuals and their companies.

Thank you .

Sincerely,

_____

Sample Short Complaint Letter To The Federal Trade Commission

Date: _____

Federal Trade Commission

_____

_____

Dear Sir or Madam:

I am having difficulties with several companies and request that you immediately send to me all of the proper forms so that I may file a complaint with your agency about violations of the following two federal laws:

The Fair Debt collections Practices Act
The Fair Credit Reporting Act

Thank you for your prompt response to this request.

Sincerely,

_____

FTC Complaint Form

This form is available for you to send a complaint to the Federal Trade Commission concerning a particular company or organization. Although the Commission cannot resolve individual problems for consumers, it can act against a company if it sees a pattern of possible law violations.

Remember that the FTC may share the information you provide with others. If you would like to forward unsolicited commercial e-mail (spam) to the Commission, please send it directly to UCE@FTC.GOV without using this form.

How Do We Reach You?

First Name: _____

Last Name: _____

Street Address: _____

City: _____

State: _____ Zip: _____

Country: _____

E-Mail Address: _____

Home Phone: _____

Work Phone:_____

Tell Us Your Complaint:

_____

_____

_____

_____

_____

_____

_____

_____

_____

_____

_____

_____

Subject of Your Complaint: (i.e., Multi-Level Marketing, Automobile, etc.)

Name of Company You Are Complaining About:

Street Address: _____

City: _____

State: _____

Country: _____

FTC Complaint Form

Zip Code or Postal Code: _____

Company Web Site: _____

Company E-Mail Address: _____

Phone Number: _____

How Did the Company Initially Contact You?

( ) In Person ( ) Fax ( ) Internet Web Site

( ) E-Mail ( ) Mail ( ) Phone ( ) Print

(   )   TV   /   Radio   (   )   (Other):

How Much Did the Company Ask You To Pay?

$ _____

How Much Did You Actually Pay the Company?

$ _____

How Did You Pay the Company?

( ) Check (Personal) ( ) Bank Money Order

( ) Postal Money Order ( ) Certified Check

( ) Other: _____

Representative or Salesperson

First Name _____

Last Name: _____

Date Company Contacted You:
 (MM/DD/YYYY): _____

Briefly Explain Your Problem:

_____

_____

_____

_____

A Checklist When Your Identity's Been Stolen

❑ Contact the fraud departments of the three major credit bureaus to flag your file with a fraud alert.

❑ Include a statement with the fraud department that creditors should get your permission before opening any new accounts in your name.

❑ Ask the credit bureaus for copies of your reports. Review them to make sure no additional fraudulent accounts have been opened in your name.

❑ In a few months, order new copies of your reports to verify your revisions and changes, and make sure no new fraudulent activity has occurred.

❑ Contact creditors for any accounts that have been tampered with or opened fraudulently. Ask to speak with someone in the security or fraud department, and follow up in writing.

❑ File a report with your local police

❑ If an identity thief has stolen your mail for access to new credit cards, etc., report it to your local postal inspector.

❑ When you open a new account, ask that a password is used before any inquiries or changes can be made on the account. Avoid using easily available information.

❑ If you discover that an identity thief has changed the billing address on an existing credit card account or accessed your checking account, close the account.

❑ If an identity thief has established new phone service in your name or is making unauthorized calls that appear to come from and are billed to your cellular phone, cancel the account.

❑ If someone is using your SSN when applying for a job, contact Social Security Administration (SSA) to verify the accuracy of your reported earnings and that your name is recorded correctly.

❑ If you suspect your name or SSN is being used to get a driver's license, report it to your DMV. If your state uses your SSN as your driver's license number, ask to subscribe another number.

Appendix B—Action Chart

Chart Your Course Of Action

Use this form to record the steps you've taken to report the fraudulent use of your identity. Keep this list in a safe place.

Credit Bureaus—Report Fraud

Bureau	Phone Number	Date Contacted	Contact Person	Comments
Equifax	1-800-525-6285			
Experian	1-888-397-3742			
Trans Union	1-800-680-7289			

Books, Credit Card Issuers and Other Creditors (Contact each creditor promptly to protect your legal rights.)

Creditor	Address & Phone Number	Date Contacted	Contact Person	Comments

Law Enforcement Authorities—Report Identity Theft

Bureau	Phone Number	Date Contacted	Contact Person	Report Number	Comments
Federal Trade Commission	1-877-IDTHEFT				
Local Police Dept.					

Appendix C—Helpful Organizations

The Privacy Rights Clearinghouse
Beth Givens, Project Director
1717 Kettner Ave. Suite 105
San Diego, CA 92101
Voice: (619) 298-3396; Fax: (619) 298-5681
E-mail: prc@privacyrights.org ; http://www.privacyrights.org

The Privacy Rights Clearinghouse is a nonprofit consumer information and advocacy program. It offers consumers a unique opportunity to learn how to protect their personal privacy.

The PRC was established in 1992 with funding from the Telecommunications Education Trust, a program of the California Public Utilities Commission. From 1992 through October 1996, the PRC was administered by the Center for Public Interest Law of the University of San Diego School of Law.

Center for Media Education.
1511 K Street, NW Suite 518,
Washington, DC 20005.
(202) 628-2620. Fax: (202) 628-2554
Email: cme@cme.org.

A national non-profit organization dedicated to improving the quality of electronic media, especially on the behalf of children and families.

Consumer Project on Technology
Box 19367, Washington, DC
20036, (202) 387-8030 (tel), (202) 234-5176 (fax)

The CPT was created by Ralph Nader in the Spring of 1995. It focuses on a variety of issues, including telecommunications regulation; fair use under the copyright law; issues relating to the pricing, ownership and development of pharmaceutical drugs; impact of technology on personal privacy; and several other issues.

Electronic Privacy Information Center
666 Pennsylvania Ave., SE
 Suite 301, Washington, DC 20003.
(202) 544 9240, FAX: (202) 547 5482
www.epic.org; e-mail: info@epic.org.

EPIC is a public interest research center in Washington, D.C. It was established in 1994 to focus public attention on emerging civil liberties issues and to protect privacy, the First Amendment, and constitutional values.
Contact Information:

The NAMEDA
P.O. Box 53326
Washington, DC 20009
(703) 908-9125; FAX: (703) 908-0186;
Email: info (@named.org).

A non-profit grass roots organization, founded by America's leading privacy advocates, dedicated to protecting your private data from being sold by others without your consent.

Communications Fraud Control Organization
3030 N. Central Avenue, Suite 804,
Phoenix, AZ 85012
602-265-CFCA (2322) Fax: 602-265-1015;
e-mail: fraud@cfca.org

Founded in 1985, CFCA is a not-for-profit international educational association working to help combat telecommunications fraud. CFCA seeks to promote a close association among telecom security personnel, to enhance their professional status and efficiency, and to serve as a clearinghouse of information pertaining to the fraudulent use of telecommunications services.

Electronic Frontier Foundation (EFF).
P.O. Box 170190
San Francisco, CA 94117; **www.eff.org**;
(415) 668-7171; FAX: (415) 668-7007.

EFF was founded in July 1990 as a non-profit public interest group focused on protecting civil liberties, privacy, free expression, and access to public resources and information online, in addition to promoting responsibility in cyberspace.

Fraud Index
222 Purchase Street, Suite 201
Rye, NY 10580 FAX: 914-690-1170;
www.fraudindex.com

An E-Newsletter, delivered directly to your e-mail every week about fraud. Their editorial staff maintains a constant watch for the most important fraud stories of the day. This invaluable service has access to hundreds of sources worldwide, all on the subject of fraud.

American Association of Retired Persons (AARP)
Consumer Issues Section
601 E Street, NW
Washington, DC 20049
202-434-6030; Fax: 202-434-6466

AARP's Consumer Issues Section advocates on behalf of mid-life and older consumers, develops and distributes consumer information, and educates the private sector about the specific needs of older consumers. Programs and materials on housing, insurance, funeral practices, eligibility for public benefits, financial security, transportation and consumer protection issues are developed, with special focus on the needs and problems of older consumers.

Coalition Against Insurance Fraud
1511 K Street, NW, Suite 623
Washington, DC 20005
202-393-7330
Fax: 202-393-7329
Web site: **www.InsuranceFraud.org**

The Coalition Against Insurance Fraud is a national alliance of consumer groups, government agencies, and insurance companies dedicated to combating all forms of insurance fraud through advocacy and public information. It conducts research and develops public education programs and publishes a consumer brochure, *How to Avoid Becoming a Victim of Insurance Fraud*, which is available on request. It also refers consumers to appropriate agencies to report incidences of insurance fraud.

Consumer Action
717 Market Street, Suite 310

San Francisco, CA 94103
415-777-9635
(consumer complaint hotline, 10 a.m.—2 p.m., PST)
213-624-8327 (hotline)
Fax: 415-777-5267
E-mail: info@consumer-action.org

Consumer Action assists consumers with marketplace problems. An education and advocacy organization specializing in credit, finance and telecommunications issues, Consumer Action offers a multi-lingual consumer complaint hotline, free information on its surveys of banks and long-distance telephone companies, and consumer education materials in as many as eight languages.

National Consumer Law Center (NCLC)
18 Tremont Street
Boston, MA 02108
617-523-8010; Fax: 617-523-7398
Web site: **www.consumerlaw.org;**
E-mail: consumerlaw@nclc.org

NCLC is an advocacy and research organization focusing on the needs of low-income consumers. It represents the interests of consumers in court, before administrative agencies, and before legislatures. The Center also publishes *Surviving Debt: A Guide for Consumers* and the *Consumer Credit and Sales Legal Practice Series* consisting of thirteen desk reference manuals for attorneys.

National Consumers League (NCL)
1701 K Street, NW
Suite 1200
Washington, DC 20006
202-835-3323; Fax: 202-835-0747

Web site: **www.natlconsumersleague.org;**
E-mail: nclncl@aol.com

Founded in 1899, the NCL is America's pioneer consumer advocacy organization. The league is a nonprofit membership organization working for health, safety and fairness in the marketplace and workplace. Current principal issue areas include consumer fraud, food and drug safety, fair labor standards, child labor, health care, the environment, financial services and telecommunications. The league develops and distributes consumer education materials and newsletters.

National Fraud Information Center (NFIC)
P.O. Box 65868
Washington, DC 20035
Toll free: 1-800-876-7060
(9 a.m.—8 p.m. M-F EST; TDD available)
Fax: 202-835-0767; TDD/TTY: 202-835-0778
Web site: **www.fraud.org;** E-mail: fraudinfo@psinet.com

NFIC assists consumers with recognizing and filing complaints about telemarketing and Internet fraud. A project of the National Consumers League, the center has a toll-free hotline that provides consumers with information to help them avoid becoming victims of fraud, referral to appropriate law enforcement agencies and professional associations, and assistance in filing complaints. The center also provides professionals involved in consumer fraud prevention and enforcement with telecommunications systems and data links to improve fraud regulation, prevention and law enforcement. Spanish-speaking counselors available.

Privacy International
666 Penn Avenue, SE, Suite 301

Washington, DC 20003
E-mail: pi@privacy.org; Website: **www.privacy.org**

An international human rights group based in London, England, with offices in Washington, DC and Sydney, Australia. PI has members in over 40 countries and campaigns against video surveillance and other privacy violations in many countries including Australia, United Kingdom and the Philippines.

Appendix D—Internet Privacy Resources & Products

Organizations

Association for Interactive Media (AIM)
http://www.interactivehq.org
AIM is the non-profit trade association for business users of the Internet. Its members are companies that are committed to maximizing the value of the Net to businesses and consumers. AIM's mission centers on these three important areas: 1) Defending the industry in Washington; 2) Promoting consumer confidence; and 3) Providing business-to-business networking opportunities.

Center for Democracy and Technology
http://www.cdt.org/privacy/—Data Privacy
http://www.cdt.org/privacy/guide/—Guide to Online Privacy
The Center for Democracy and Technology works to promote democratic values and constitutional liberties in the digital age. With expertise in law, technology, and policy, CDT seeks practical solutions to enhance free expression and privacy in global communications technologies. CDT is dedicated to building consensus among all parties interested in the future of the Internet and other new communications media.

Consumer.net
http://consumer.net/index.asp

Consumer.net is the consumer information organization, providing helpful links and information on consumer privacy, including state-specific policies.

Internet PRIVACY Coalition

http://www.crypto.org/

The mission of the Internet Privacy Coalition is to promote privacy and security on the Internet through widespread public availability of strong encryption and the relaxation of export controls on cryptography.

Network Advertising Initiative

http://www.networkadvertising.org/

NAI is a group of third party network advertisers who are committed to increasing consumer confidence and contributing to the growth of electronic commerce. NAI's principal business is delivering targeted advertising that can be tailored to consumers' declared or predicted characteristics or preferences. NAI is committed to providing consumers with a clear explanation of what data they collect, how they use it, and why use of data can benefit consumers' experience online.

Online Privacy Alliance

http://www.privacyalliance.org/

The Online Privacy Alliance is a diverse group of corporations and associations who have come together to introduce and promote business-wide actions that create an environment of trust and foster the protection of individuals' privacy online.

Privacy and American Business

http://www.pandab.org/

Privacy & American Business is the activity of the non-profit Center for Social & Legal Research. Since its launch in 1993, P&AB has become the leading authoritative source for tracking new business-privacy issues and for promoting voluntary, balanced consumer privacy policies and practices, nationally and internationally. Its surveys, undertaken by Louis Harris & Associates and other prestigious survey organizations, document what consumers want in business services and also what concerns they have about safeguarding their personal data.

Privacy.org—Organization that informs consumers about privacy issues.

http://www.privacy.org

Providing news, resources, and tips for Privacy Action, this organization is a useful tool for informing consumers about privacy issues.

The Privacy Place

http://www.privacy.org/

Providing news, resources, and tips for Privacy Action, this organization is a useful tool for informing consumers about privacy issues.

U.S. Consumer Gateway

http://www.consumer.gov/

Consumer.gov—is a "one-stop" link to a broad range of federal information resources available online. It is designed so that you can locate information by category—such as Food, Health, Product Safety, Your Money, and Transportation. Each category has subcategories to direct you to areas within individual federal web sites containing related information.

CPA WebTrust

http://www.cpawebtrust.org/

With the CPA WebTrust Program, a specially licensed Certified Public Accountant examines a company's Web site to ensure that its Web transactions meet the program's accepted high standards in three key areas: Information Protection, Business Practices, Transaction Integrity.

Privacy Products for Consumers

Junkbusters

http://www.junkbusters.com/

Junkbusters is one of the world's most comprehensive collections of information about junk messages and how to stop them. The Internet

Junkbuster helps you control commercial communications to your Web browser and give you new ways to use your browser to control other kinds of junk.

Net Nanny

http://www.netnanny.com/

Net Nanny provides families and businesses with a high degree of digital privacy and protection by placing control of data security in the hands of authorized users using innovative technology solutions

Privacy, INC.—Software that rates a site's privacy standards based on a 1-4 star system.

http://www.privacyinc.com

Privacy, Inc.'s Consumer Privacy Guide provides concise details of who are capturing information about you, how, why, and what can you do about it. Also included are details regarding how your company may be monitoring your activity, both inside & even outside the workplace.

Safe Consumer

http://www.safeconsumer.org/

Safe Consumer protects both Internet users and Web site owners, through a program which objectively reviews and audits online businesses and organizations to ensure what everyone in the online community needs and demands: privacy, security and integrity.

Zero Knowledge

http://www.zeroknowledge.com/

Zero-Knowledge Systems Inc. is dedicated to providing customers with the tools to protect their privacy and freedom while on the Internet. The nature of the Internet and the diverse international make up of its citizens dictates that protecting privacy with multi-jurisdictional legislation and mediocre security will not provide true privacy nor security. True privacy and security on the Internet can only be assured with mathematics, cryptography and source code.

Appendix E—Federal Trade Commission Regional Offices

The Northwest Region serves the residents of the following states:

Alaska, Idaho, Montana, Oregon, Washington and Wyoming.

The FTC has developed resource guides to help consumers find the appropriate agencies to contact about consumer-related matters. These guides contain lists of nonprofit, state and local agencies for the states listed above.

The address is:

> **Northwest Region**
> **Federal Trade Commission**
> **2896 Federal Building, 915 Second Avenue**
> **Seattle, WA 98174.**

For Consumer Complaints contact the Consumer Response Center:

By phone: toll free 877-FTC-HELP (382-4357); 9:00 am to 5:00 p.m. Eastern Standard Time, Monday through Friday;

The Southeast Region serves the residents of the following states:

Alabama, Florida, Georgia, Mississippi, North Carolina, South Carolina, and Tennessee.

The FTC has developed resource guides to help consumers find the appropriate agencies to contact about consumer-related matters. These guides contain lists of nonprofit, state and local agencies for the states listed above.

The address is:

> **Southeast Region**
> **Federal Trade Commission**
> **Suite 5M35**
> **60 Forsyth Street, SW**
> **Atlanta, GA 30303-2322.**

For Consumer Complaints contact the Consumer Response Center:

By phone: toll free 877-FTC-HELP (382-4357); 9:00 am to 5:00 p.m. Eastern Standard Time, Monday through Friday.

By mail: Consumer Response Center, Federal Trade Commission, 600 Pennsylvania Ave, NW, Washington, DC 20580.

The Western Region has two offices serving the residents of the following states:

Arizona, Northern California, Southern California, Colorado, Hawaii, Nevada and Utah.

The FTC has developed resource guides to help consumers find the appropriate agencies to contact about consumer-related matters. These guides contain lists of nonprofit, state and local agencies for the states listed above.

The addresses are:

Western Region
Federal Trade Commission
901 Market Street, Suite 570
San Francisco, CA 94103

Western Region
Federal Trade Commission
10877 Wilshire Blvd., Suite 700
Los Angeles, California 90024

For Consumer Complaints contact the Consumer Response Center:

By phone: toll free 877-FTC-HELP (382-4357); 9:00 am to 5:00 p.m. Eastern Standard Time, Monday through Friday.

By mail: Consumer Response Center, Federal Trade Commission, 600 Pennsylvania Ave, NW, Washington, DC 20580

The Northeast Region serves the residents of the following states:

Connecticut, Maine, Massachusetts, New Hampshire, New Jersey, New York, Rhode Island, and Vermont.

The FTC has developed resource guides to help consumers find the appropriate agencies to contact about consumer-related matters. These guides contain lists of nonprofit, state and local agencies for the states listed above.

The address is:

> Northeast Region
> Federal Trade Commission
> 1 Bowling Green
> New York, NY 10004.

For Consumer Complaints contact the Consumer Response Center:

By phone: toll free 877-FTC-HELP (382-4357); 9:00 am to 5:00 p.m. Eastern Standard Time, Monday through Friday.

By mail: Consumer Response Center, Federal Trade Commission, 600 Pennsylvania Ave, NW, Washington, DC 20580

Appendix F—Federal Government Resources

Federal Government

Federal Trade Commission (FTC)—www.ftc.gov The FTC is the federal clearinghouse for complaints by victims of identity theft. Although the FTC does not have the authority to bring criminal cases, the Commission helps victims of identity theft by providing them with information to help resolve the financial and other problems that can result from identity theft. The FTC also may refer victim complaints to other appropriate government agencies and private organizations for action.

If you've been a victim of identity theft, file a complaint with the FTC by contacting the FTC's Identity Theft Hotline by telephone: toll-free 1-877-IDTHEFT (438-4338); TDD: 202-326-2502; by mail:

> **Identity Theft Clearinghouse**
> Federal Trade Commission
> 600 Pennsylvania Avenue, NW
> Washington, DC 20580; or online: **www.consumer.gov/idtheft**

Banking Agencies

If you're having trouble getting your financial institution to help you resolve your banking-related identity theft problems including problems with bank-issued credit cards contact the agency with the appropriate jurisdiction. If you're not sure which agency has jurisdiction over your institution, call your bank or visit **www.ffiec.gov/nic/default.htm**

Federal Deposit Insurance Corporation (FDIC)—www.fdic.gov
The FDIC supervises state-chartered banks that are not members of the Federal Reserve System and insures deposits at banks and savings and loans. Call the FDIC Consumer Call Center at 1-800-934-3342; or write:

> Federal Deposit Insurance Corporation
> Division of Compliance and Consumer Affairs
> 550 17th Street, NW,
> Washington, DC 20429.

Federal Reserve System (Fed)—www.federalreserve.gov The Fed supervises state-chartered banks that are members of the Federal Reserve System. Call: 202-452-3693; or write:

> **Division of Consumer and Community Affairs**
> Mail Stop 801, Federal Reserve Board
> Washington, DC 20551

Or contact the Federal Reserve Bank in your area. The 12 Reserve Banks are located in Boston, New York City, Philadelphia, Cleveland, Richmond, Atlanta, Chicago, St. Louis, Minneapolis, Kansas City, Dallas and San Francisco.

National Credit Union Administration (NCUA) — www.ncua.gov The NCUA charters and supervises federal credit unions and insures deposits at federal credit unions and many state credit unions. Call: 703-518-6360; or write:

> Compliance Officer
> National Credit Union Administration
> 1775 Duke Street
> Alexandria, VA 22314

Office of the Comptroller of the Currency (OCC)—www.occ.treas.gov The OCC charters and supervises national banks. If the word "national" appears in the name of a bank, or the initials "N.A." follow its name, the OCC oversees its operations.

Call: 1-800-613-6743 (business days 9:00 a.m. to 4:00 p.m. CST); fax: 713-336-4301; write:

> **Customer Assistance Group**
> 1301 McKinney Street, Suite 3710
> Houston, TX 77010
> or e-mail: Customer.Assistance@occ.treas.gov

Office of Thrift Supervision (OTS)—www.ots.treas.gov The OTS is the primary regulator of all federal and many state-chartered thrift institutions, which include savings banks and savings and loan institutions.

Call 202-906-6000; or write:

> **Office of Thrift Supervision**
> 1700 G Street, NW
> Washington, DC 20552.

Department of Justice (DOJ) —www.usdoj.gov

The DOJ and its U.S. Attorneys prosecute federal identity theft cases. Information on identity theft is available at **www.usdoj.gov/criminal/fraud/idtheft.html**

Federal Bureau of Investigation (FBI)—www.fbi.gov

The FBI is one of the federal criminal law enforcement agencies that investigates cases of identity theft. Local field offices are listed in the Blue Pages of your telephone directory.

Federal Communications Commission (FCC)—www.fcc.gov

The FCC regulates interstate and international communications by radio, television, wire, satellite and cable. The FCC's Consumer

Information Bureau is the consumer's one-stop source for information, forms, applications and current issues before the FCC.

Call: 1-888-CALL-FCC; TTY: 1-888-TELL-FCC; or write:

Federal Communications Commission
Consumer Information Bureau
445 12th Street, SW, Room 5A863
Washington, DC 20554.

You can file complaints via the online complaint form at www.fcc.gov, or e-mail questions to fccinfo@fcc.gov.

You can file a complaint with the FTC by contacting the Consumer Response Center by phone: toll-free 1-877-FTC-HELP (382-4357); TDD: 202-326-2502; by mail:

Consumer Response Center
Federal Trade Commission
600 Pennsylvania Ave., NW
Washington, DC 20580

Or through the Internet, using the online complaint form. Although the Commission cannot resolve individual problems for consumers, it can act against a company if it sees a pattern of possible law violations.

Internal Revenue Service (IRS)—www.treas.gov/irs/ci

The IRS is responsible for administering and enforcing the internal revenue laws. If you believe someone has assumed your identity to file federal Income Tax Returns, or to commit other tax fraud, call toll-free: 1-800-829-0433.

U.S. Secret Service (USSS)—www.treas.gov/usss

The U.S. Secret Service is one of the federal law enforcement agencies that investigates financial crimes, which may include identity theft. Although the Secret Service generally investigates cases where the dollar loss is substantial, your information may provide evidence of a larger pattern of fraud requiring their involvement. Local field offices are listed in the Blue Pages of your telephone directory.

Social Security Administration (SSA)—www.ssa.gov

SSA may assign you a new SSN at your request if you continue to experience problems even after trying to resolve the problems resulting from identity theft. SSA field office employees work closely with victims of identity theft and third parties to collect the evidence needed to assign a new SSN in these cases.

SSA Office of the Inspector General *(SSA/OIG)*

The SSA/OIG is one of the federal law enforcement agencies that investigates cases of identity theft.

Direct allegations that an SSN has been stolen or misused to the SSA Fraud Hotline. Call: 1-800- 269-0271; fax: 410-597-0018; or write:

> **SSA Fraud Hotline**
> P.O. Box 17768
> Baltimore, MD 21235
> E-mail: oig.hotline@ssa.gov

**U.S. Postal Inspection Service (USPIS)—
www.usps.gov/websites/depart/inspect**

The USPIS is one of the federal law enforcement agencies that investigates cases of identity theft. USPIS is the law enforcement arm of the U.S. Postal Service. USPIS has primary jurisdiction in all matters infringing on the integrity of the U.S. mail. You can locate the USPIS district office nearest you by calling your local post office or checking the list at the web site above.

U.S. Securities and Exchange Commission (SEC)—www.sec.gov

The SEC's Office of Investor Education and Assistance serves investors who complain to the SEC about investment fraud or the mishandling of their investments by securities professionals. If you've experienced identity theft in connection with a securities transaction, write:

SEC
450 Fifth Street, NW
Washington, DC, 20549-0213
You also may call 202-942-7040
or send an e-mail to help@sec.gov.

U. S. Trustee (UST) — www.usdoj.gov/ust

if you believe someone has filed for bankruptcy using your name, write to the U.S. Trustee in the region where the bankruptcy was filed. Lists of the U.S. Trustee's Regional Offices is available on the UST web site, or check the Blue Pages of your phone book under U.S. Government Bankruptcy Administration. Your letter should describe the situation and provide proof of your identity. The U.S. Trustee, if appropriate, will make a criminal referral to criminal law enforcement authorities if you provide appropriate documentation to substantiate your claim. You also may want to file a complaint with the U.S. Attorney and/or the FBI in the city where the bankruptcy was filed.

The U.S. Trustee does not provide legal representation, legal advice or referrals to lawyers. That means you may need to hire an attorney to help convince the bankruptcy court that the filing is fraudulent. The U.S. Trustee does not provide consumers with copies of court documents. Those documents are available from the bankruptcy clerk's office for a fee.

State and Local Governments

Many states and local governments have passed laws related to identity theft; others may be considering such legislation. Where specific identity theft laws do not exist, the practices may be prohibited under other laws. Contact your State Attorney General's office (for a list of state offices, visit **www.naag.org**) or local consumer protection agency

to find out whether your state has laws related to identity theft, or visit
www.consumer.gov/idtheft/

National Telecommunications and Information Administration
http://www.ntia.doc.gov/

The National Telecommunications and Information Administration
(NTIA), an agency of the U.S. Department of Commerce, is the
Executive Branch's principal voice on domestic and international
telecommunications and information technology issues. NTIA works
to spur innovation, encourage competition, help create jobs and provide consumers with more choices and better quality telecommunications products and services at lower prices.

Department of Education: Parents Guide to the Internet
http://www.ed.gov/pubs/parents/internet/

U.S. Department of Education, the Office of Educational Research and
Improvement, and the Office of Educational Technology present a site
offering advice to parents on how the Internet should best serve children.

Appendix G—Identity Theft & Assumption Deterrence Act of 1998—

Full Text as amended by Public Law 105-318, 112 Stat. 3007 (Oct. 30, 1998)

An Act

To amend chapter 47 of title 18, United States Code, relating to identity fraud, and for other purposes. [NOTE: Oct. 30, 1998—[H.R. 4151]

Be it enacted by the Senate and House of Representatives of the United States of America in Congress assembled, [NOTE: Identity Theft and Assumption Deterrence Act of 1998.] Sec.

001. Short Title

002. Constitutional Authority to Enact this Legislation.

003. Identity Theft

004. Amendment of Federal Sentencing Guidelines for Offenses Under Section 1028

005. Centralized Complaint and Consumer Education Service for Victims of Identity Theft

006. Technical Amendments to Title 18, United States Code

007. Redaction of Ethics Reports Filed by Judicial Officers and Employees

§ 001. Short Title. [NOTE: 18 USC 1001 note.]

This Act may be cited as the "Identity Theft and Assumption Deterrence Act of 1998".

§ 002. Constitutional Authority to Enact this Legislation. [NOTE: 18 USC 1028 note.]

The constitutional authority upon which this Act rests is the power of Congress to regulate commerce with foreign nations and among the several States, and the authority to make all laws which shall be necessary and proper for carrying into execution the powers vested by the Constitution in the Government of the United States or in any department or officer thereof, as set forth in article I, section 8 of the United States Constitution.

§ 003. Identity Theft.

(a) Establishment of Offense.—Section 1028(a) of title 18, United States Code, is amended—

    (1)   in paragraph (5), by striking "or" at the end;

    (2)   in paragraph (6), by adding "or" at the end;

    (3)   in the flush matter following paragraph (6), by striking "or attempts to do so,"; and

    (4)   by inserting after paragraph (6) the following:"(7) knowingly transfers or uses, without lawful authority, a means of identification of another person with the intent to commit, or to aid or abet, any unlawful activity that constitutes a violation of Federal law, or that constitutes a felony under any applicable State or local law;".

(b) Penalties.—Section 1028(b) of title 18, United States Code, is amended—

    (1)   in paragraph (1)—

        (A)   in subparagraph (B), by striking "or" at the end;

        (B)   in subparagraph (C), by adding "or" at the end; and

(C) by adding at the end the following: "(D) an offense under paragraph (7) of such subsection that involves the transfer or use of 1 or more means of identification if, as a result of the offense, any individual committing the offense obtains anything of value aggregating $1,000 or more during any 1-year period;";

(2) in paragraph (2)—

(A) in subparagraph (A), by striking "or transfer of an identification document or" and inserting ", transfer, or use of a means of identification, an identification document, or a"; and

(B) in subparagraph (B), by inserting "or (7)" after "(3)";

(3) by amending paragraph (3) to read as follows: "(3) a fine under this title or imprisonment for not more than 20 years, or both, if the offense is committed—

"(A) to facilitate a drug trafficking crime (as defined in section 929(a)(2));

"(B) in connection with a crime of violence (as defined in section 924(c)(3)); or

"(C) after a prior conviction under this section becomes final;";

(4) in paragraph (4), by striking "and" at the end;

(5) by redesignating paragraph (5) as paragraph (6); and

(6) by inserting after paragraph (4) the following: "(5) in the case of any offense under subsection (a), forfeiture to the United States of any personal property used or intended to be used to commit the offense; and".

(c) Circumstances.—Section 1028(c) of title 18, United States Code, is amended by striking paragraph (3) and inserting the following:

"(3) either—

"(A) the production, transfer, possession, or use prohibited by this section is in or affects interstate or foreign commerce; or

"(B) the means of identification, identification document, false identification document, or document- making implement is transported in the mail in the course of the production, transfer, possession, or use prohibited by this section.".

(d) Definitions.—Subsection (d) of section 1028 of title 18, United States Code, is amended to read as follows:

"(d) In this section—

"(1) the term 'document-making implement' means any implement, impression, electronic device, or computer hardware or software, that is specifically configured or primarily used for making an identification document, a false identification document, or another document-making implement;

"(2) the term `identification document' means a document made or issued by or under the authority of the United States Government, a State, political subdivision of a State, a foreign government, political subdivision of a foreign government, an international governmental or an international quasi-governmental organization which, when completed with information concerning a particular individual, is of a type intended or commonly accepted for the purpose of identification of individuals;

"(3) the term `means of identification' means any name or number that may be used, alone or in conjunction with any other information, to identify a specific individual, including any—

"(A) name, social security number, date of birth, official State or government issued driver's license or identification number, alien registration number, government passport number, employer or taxpayer identification number;

"(B) unique biometric data, such as fingerprint, voice print, retina or iris image, or other unique physical representation;

"(C) unique electronic identification number, address, or routing code; or

"(D) telecommunication identifying information or access device (as defined in section 1029(e));

"(4) the term 'personal identification card' means an identification document issued by a State or local government solely for the purpose of identification;

"(5) the term 'produce' includes alter, authenticate, or assemble; and

"(6) the term 'State' includes any State of the United States, the District of Columbia, the Commonwealth of Puerto Rico, and any other commonwealth, possession, or territory of the United States.".

(e) Attempt and Conspiracy.—Section 1028 of title 18, United States Code, is amended by adding at the end the following:

"(f) Attempt and Conspiracy.—Any person who attempts or conspires to commit any offense under this section shall be subject to the same penalties as those prescribed for the offense, the commission of which was the object of the attempt or conspiracy.".

(f) Forfeiture Procedures.—Section 1028 of title 18, United States Code, is amended by adding at the end the following:

"(g) Forfeiture Procedures.—The forfeiture of property under this section, including any seizure and disposition of the property and any related judicial or administrative proceeding, shall be governed by the provisions of section 413 (other than subsection (d) of that section) of the Comprehensive Drug Abuse Prevention and Control Act of 1970 (21 U.S.C. 853).".

(g) Rule of Construction.—Section 1028 of title 18, United States Code, is amended by adding at the end the following:

"(h) Rule of Construction.—For purpose of subsection (a)(7), a single identification document or false identification document that contains 1 or more means of identification shall be construed to be 1 means of identification.".

(h) Conforming Amendments.—Chapter 47 of title 18, United States Code, is amended—

(1)   in the heading for section 1028, by adding "and information" at the end; and

(2)   in the table of sections at the beginning of the chapter, in the item relating to section 1028, by adding "and information" at the end.

§ 004. Amendment of Federal Sentencing Guidelines for Offenses Under Section 1028. [NOTE: 28 USC 994 note.]

(a)   In General.—Pursuant to its authority under section 994(p) of title 28, United States Code, the United States Sentencing Commission shall review and amend the Federal sentencing guidelines and the policy statements of the Commission, as appropriate, to provide an appropriate penalty for each offense under section 1028 of title 18, United States Code, as amended by this Act.

(b) Factors for Consideration.—In carrying out subsection (a), the United States Sentencing Commission shall consider, with respect to each offense described in subsection (a)—

(1)   the extent to which the number of victims (as defined in section 3663A(a) of title 18, United States Code) involved in the offense, including harm to reputation, inconvenience, and other difficulties resulting from the offense, is an adequate measure for establishing penalties under the Federal sentencing guidelines;

(2)   the number of means of identification, identification documents, or false identification documents (as those terms are defined in section 1028(d) of title 18, United States Code, as amended by this Act) involved in the offense, is an adequate measure for establishing penalties under the Federal sentencing guidelines;

(3)   the extent to which the value of the loss to any individual caused by the offense is an adequate measure for establishing penalties under the Federal sentencing guidelines;

(4)   the range of conduct covered by the offense;

(5)   the extent to which sentencing enhancements within the Federal sentencing guidelines and the court's authority to sentence above the applicable guideline range are adequate to ensure punishment at or near the maximum penalty for the most egregious conduct covered by the offense;

(6)   the extent to which Federal sentencing guidelines sentences for the offense have been constrained by statutory maximum penalties;

(7)   the extent to which Federal sentencing guidelines for the offense adequately achieve the purposes of sentencing

set forth in section 3553(a)(2) of title 18, United States Code; and

(8)   any other factor that the United States Sentencing Commission considers to be appropriate.

§ 005. Centralized Complaining and Consumer Education Service for Victims of Identity Theft. [NOTE: 18 USC 1028 note.]

(a) In General. —Not later than 1 year after the date of enactment of this Act, the Federal Trade Commission shall establish procedures to—

    (1)   log and acknowledge the receipt of complaints by individuals who certify that they have a reasonable belief that 1 or more of their means of identification (as defined in section 1028 of title 18, United States Code, as amended by this Act) have been assumed, stolen, or otherwise unlawfully acquired in violation of section 1028 of title 18, United States Code, as amended by this Act;

    (2)   provide informational materials to individuals described in paragraph (1); and

    (3)   refer complaints described in paragraph (1) to appropriate entities, which may include referral to—

        (A)   the 3 major national consumer reporting agencies; and

        (B)   appropriate law enforcement agencies for potential law enforcement action.

(b) Authorization of Appropriations.—There are authorized to be appropriated such sums as may be necessary to carry out this section.

§ 006. Technical Amendments to Title 18, United States Code.

(a) Technical Correction Relating to Criminal Forfeiture Procedures.—Section 982(b)(1) of title 18, United States Code, is amended to read as follows: "(1) The forfeiture of property under this section, including any seizure and disposition of the property and any related judicial or administrative proceeding, shall be governed by the provisions of section 413 (other than subsection (d) of that section) of the Comprehensive Drug Abuse Prevention and Control Act of 1970 (21 U.S.C. 853).".

(b) Economic Espionage and Theft of Trade Secrets as Predicate Offenses for Wire Interception.—Section 2516(1)(a) of title 18, United States Code, is amended by inserting "chapter 90 (relating to protection of trade secrets)," after "to espionage),".

§ 007. Redaction of Ethics Reports Filed by Judicial Officers and Employees.

Section 105(b) of the Ethics in Government Act of 1978 (5 U.S.C. App.) is amended by adding at the end the following new paragraph:

"(3)(A) This section does not require the immediate and unconditional availability of reports filed by an individual described in section 109(8) or 109(10) of this Act if a finding is made by the Judicial Conference, in consultation with United States Marshall Service, that revealing personal and sensitive information could endanger that individual.

"(B) A report may be redacted pursuant to this paragraph only—

"(i) to the extent necessary to protect the individual who filed the report; and

"(ii) for as long as the danger to such individual exists.

"(C) The Administrative Office of the United States Courts shall submit to the Committees on the Judiciary of the House of Representatives and of the Senate an annual report with respect to the operation of this paragraph including—

  "(i) the total number of reports redacted pursuant to this paragraph;

  "(ii) the total number of individuals whose reports have been redacted pursuant to this paragraph; and

  "(iii) the types of threats against individuals whose reports are redacted, if appropriate.

"(D) The Judicial Conference, in consultation with the Department of Justice, shall issue regulations setting forth the circumstances under which redaction is appropriate under this paragraph and the procedures for redaction.[NOTE: Regulations.]

"(E) This paragraph shall expire on December 31, 2001, and apply to filings through calendar year 2001.". [NOTE: Expiration date.]

Approved October 30, 1998.

LEGISLATIVE HISTORY—H.R. 4151 (S. 512):

SENATE REPORTS: No. 105-274 accompanying S. 512 (Comm. on the Judiciary).

CONGRESSIONAL RECORD, Vol. 144 (1998):

 Oct. 7, considered and passed House.

 Oct. 14, considered and passed Senate.

WEEKLY COMPILATION OF PRESIDENTIAL DOCUMENTS, Vol. 34 (1998):

 Oct. 30, Presidential statement.

Appendix H—Privacy
Act of 1974

Privacy Act of 1974

(PL 93-5795; USC 552a: 88 Stat. 1896)

Promotes greater governmental respect for the privacy of citizens. It has been amended by:

- ❖ PL 94–183; December 31, 1975; 89 Stat. 1057
- ❖ PL 97–365; October 25, 1982; 96 Stat. 1749
- ❖ PL 97–375; December 21, 1982; 96 Stat. 1821
- ❖ PL 97–452; January 12, 1983; 96 Stat. 2478
- ❖ PL 98–497; October 19, 1984; 98 Stat. 2292
- ❖ PL 100–503; October 18, 1988; 102 Stat. 2507
- ❖ PL 101–56; July 19, 1989; 103 Stat. 149

The act requires federal agencies to adopt minimum standards for the collection and processing of personal information and to publish detailed descriptions of these procedures. It also limits the making of such records available to other public and private agencies or parties and requires agencies to make records on individuals available to them upon request, subject to certain conditions and exclusions.

The Act has four basic policy objectives:

1. To restrict disclosures of personally identifiable records
2. to grant individuals more rights to access records agencies maintain on them
3. To grant individuals the right to seek amendments to agency records maintained on themselves
4. To establish a code of "fair information practices" which requires agencies to comply with statutory norms for collection, maintenance, and dissemination of records

Personal information shall no t be collected by a collector for inclusion in a record or in a generally available publication unless:

❖ The information is collected for a lawful purpose directly related to a function or activity of the collector;
❖ The collection of the information is necessary for, or directly related to, that purpose. Personal information means information or an opinion (including information or an opinion forming part of a database), whether true or not, and whether recorded in a material form or not, about an individual whose identity is apparent, or can reasonably be ascertained, from the information or opinion.

Any personal record must be safeguarded in accordance with Privacy Act procedures.

Note: Explanations are merely to acquaint you with the law and are not meant as legal interpretations.

Appendix I—Right to Financial Privacy Act (12 U.S.C. 3401 et seq.)

The Right to Financial Privacy Act was Congress' response to a U.S. Supreme Court decision that found bank customers had no legal right of privacy for their financial information held by financial institutions. The law is largely procedural and requires government agencies to provide notice and an opportunity to object before a bank or other institution can disclose personal financial information to a government agency, usually for law enforcement purposes. The law was amended in the latter 1980s to allow postponement of notice in investigations dealing with drug trafficking and espionage.

3401. Definitions

For the purpose of this chapter, the term—

(1) "financial institution" means any office of a bank, savings bank, card issuer as defined in section 1602(n) of title 15, industrial loan company, trust company, savings association, building and loan, or homestead association (including cooperative banks), credit union, or consumer finance institution, located in any State or territory of the United States, the District of Columbia, Puerto Rico, Guam, American Samoa, or the Virgin Islands;

(2) "financial record" means an original of, a copy of, or information known to have been derived from, any record held by a financial institution pertaining to a customer's relationship with the financial institution;

(3) "Government authority" means any agency or department of the United States, or any officer, employee, or agent thereof;

(4) "person" means an individual or a partnership of five or fewer individuals;

(5) "customer" means any person or authorized representative of that person who utilized or is utilizing any service of a financial institution, or for whom a financial institution is acting or has acted as a fiduciary, in relation to an account maintained in the person's name;

(6) "holding company" means—

   (A) any bank holding company (as defined in section 1841 of this title);

   (B) any company described in section 1843(f)(1) of this title; and

   (C) any savings and loan holding company (as defined in the Home Owners' Act [12 U.S.C. 1461 et seq.]);

(7) "supervisory agency" means with respect to any particular financial institution, holding company, or any subsidiary of a financial institution or holding company, any of the following which has statutory authority to examine the financial condition, business operations, or records or transactions of that institution, holding company, or subsidiary—

   (A) the Federal Deposit Insurance Corporation;

   (B) the Director, Office of Thrift Supervision;

   (C) the National Credit Union Administration;

   (D) the Board of Governors of the Federal Reserve System;

   (E) the Comptroller of the Currency;

   (F) the Securities and Exchange Commission;

(G)   the Secretary of the Treasury, with respect to the Bank Secrecy Act [Public Law 91-508, title I) [12 U.S.C. 1951 et seq.] and subchapter II of chapter 53 of title 31; or

(H)   any State banking or securities department or agency; and

(8) "law enforcement inquiry" means a lawful investigation or official proceeding inquiring into a violation of, or failure to comply with, any criminal or civil statute or any regulation, rule, or order issued pursuant thereto.

3402. Access to financial records by Government authorities prohibited; exceptions

Except as provided by section 3403(c) or (d), 3413, or 3414 of this title, no Government authority may have access to or obtain copies of, the information contained in the financial records of any customer from a financial institution unless the financial records are reasonably described and—

(1) such customer has authorized such disclosure in accordance with section 3404 of this title;

(2) such financial records are disclosed in response to an administrative subpoena or summons which meets the requirements of section 3405 of this title;

(3) such financial records are disclosed in response to a search warrant which meets the requirements of section 3406 of this title;

(4) such financial records are disclosed in response to a judicial subpoena which meets the requirements of section 3407 of this title; or

(5) such financial records are disclosed in response to a formal written request which meets the requirements of section 3408 of this title.

3403. Confidentiality of financial records

   (a) Release of records by financial institutions prohibited

No financial institution, or officer, employee, or agent of a financial institution, may provide to any Government authority access to or copies of, or the information contained in, the financial records of any customer except in accordance with the provisions of this chapter.

   (b) Release of records upon certification of compliance with chapter

A financial institution shall not release the financial records of a customer until the Government authority seeking such records certifies in writing to the financial institution that it has complied with the applicable provisions of this chapter.

   (c) Notification to Government authority of existence of relevant information in records

Nothing in this chapter shall preclude any financial institution, or any officer, employee, or agent of a financial institution, from notifying a Government authority that such institution, or officer, employee, or agent has information which may be relevant to a possible violation of any statute or regulation. Such information may include only the name or other identifying information concerning any individual, corporation, or account involved in and the nature of any suspected illegal activity. Such information may be disclosed notwithstanding any constitution, law, or regulation of any State or political subdivision thereof to the contrary. Any financial institution, or officer, employee, or agent thereof, making a disclosure of information pursuant to this subsection, shall not be liable to the customer under any law or regulation of the United States or any constitution, law or regulation of any State or political subdivision thereof, for such disclosure or for any failure to notify the customer of such disclosure.

(d) Release of records as incident to perfection of security interest, proving a claim in bankruptcy, collecting a debt, or processing an application with regard to a Government loan, loan guarantee, etc.

    (1) Nothing in this chapter shall preclude a financial institution, as an incident to perfecting a security interest, proving a claim in bankruptcy, or otherwise collecting on a debt owing either to the financial institution itself or in its role as a fiduciary, from providing copies of any financial record to any court or Government authority.

    (2) Nothing in this chapter shall preclude a financial institution, as an incident to processing an application for assistance to a customer in the form of a Government loan, loan guaranty, or loan insurance agreement, or as an incident to processing a default on, or administering a Government guaranteed or insured loan, from initiating contact with an appropriate Government authority for the purpose of providing any financial record necessary to permit such authority to carry out its responsibilities under a loan, loan guaranty, or loan insurance agreement.

3404. Customer authorizations

(a) Statement furnished by customer to financial institution and Government authority; contents

A customer may authorize disclosure under section 3402(1) of this title if he furnishes to the financial institution and to the Government authority seeking to obtain such disclosure a signed and dated statement which—

    (1) authorizes such disclosure for a period not in excess of there months;

(2)   states that the customer may revoke such authorization at any time before the financial records are disclosed;

(3)   identifies the financial records which are authorized to be disclosed;

(4)   specifies the purposes for which, and the Government authority to which, such records may be disclosed; and

(5)   states the customer's rights under this chapter.

(b) Authorization as condition of doing business prohibited

No such authorization shall be required as a condition of doing business with any financial institution.

(c) Right of customer to access to financial institution's record of disclosures

The customer has the right, unless the Government authority obtains a court order as provided in section 3409 of this title, to obtain a copy of the record which the financial institution shall keep of all instances in which the customer's record is disclosed to a Government authority pursuant to this section, including the identity of the Government authority to which such disclosure is made.

3405. Administrative subpoena and summons

A Government authority may obtain financial records under section 3402(2) of this title pursuant to an administrative subpoena or summons otherwise authorized by law only if—

(1) there is reason to believe that the records sought are relevant to a legitimate law enforcement inquiry;

(2) a copy of the subpoena or summons has been served upon the customer or mailed to his last known address on or before the date on which the subpoena or summons was served on the financial institution together with the following notice which shall state with reasonable specificity the nature of the law enforcement inquiry:

"Records or information concerning your transactions held by the financial institution named in the attached subpoena or summons are being sought by this (agency or department) in accordance with the Right to Financial Privacy Act of 1978 [12. U.S.C. 3401 et seq.] for the following purpose: If you desire that such records or information not be made available, you must:

"1.   Fill out the accompanying motion paper and sworn statement or write one of your own, stating that you are the customer whose records are being requested by the Government and either giving the reasons you believe that the records are not relevant to the legitimate law enforcement inquiry stated in this notice or any other legal basis for objecting to the release of the records.

"2.   File the motion and statement by mailing or delivering them to the clerk of any one of the following United States district courts:

"3.   Serve the Government authority requesting the records by mailing or delivering a copy of your motion and statement to

"4.   Be prepared to come to court and present your position in further detail.

"5.   You do not need to have a lawyer, although you may wish to employ one to represent you and protect your rights.

        "If you do not follow the above procedures, upon the expiration of ten days from the date of service or fourteen days from the date of mailing of this notice, the records or information requested therein will be made available. These records may be transferred to other Government authorities for legitimate law enforcement inquiries, in which event you will be notified after the transfer."; and

(3) ten days have expired from the date of service of the notice or fourteen days have expired from the date of mailing the notice to the customer and within such time period the customer has not filed a sworn statement and motion to quash in an appropriate court, or the customer challenge provisions of section 3410 of this title have been complied with.

3406. Search warrants

(a) Applicability of Federal Rules of Criminal Procedure

A Government authority may obtain financial records under section 3402(3) of this title only if it obtains a search warrant pursuant to the Federal Rules of Criminal Procedure.

(b) Mailing of copy and notice to customer

No later than ninety days after the Government authority serves the search warrant, it shall mail to the customer's last known address a copy of the search warrant together with the following notice:

"Records or information concerning your transactions held by the financial institution named in the attached search warrant were obtained by this (agency or department) on (date) for the following purpose:

"You may have rights under the Right to Financial Privacy Act of 1978 [12 U.S.C. 3401 et. seq.]."

(c) Court-ordered delays in mailing

Upon application of the Government authority, a court may grant a delay in the mailing of the notice required in subsection (b) of this section, which delay shall not exceed one hundred and eighty days following the service of the warrant, if the court makes the findings required in section 3409(a) of this title. If the court so finds, it shall enter an ex parte order granting the requested delay and an order prohibiting the financial institution from disclosing that records have been obtained or that a search warrant for such records has been executed. Additional delays of up to ninety days may be granted by the court upon application, but only in accordance with this section. Upon expiration of the period of delay of notification of the customer, the following notice shall be mailed to the customer along with a copy of the search warrant:

"Records or information concerning your transactions held by the financial institution named in the attached search warrant were obtained by this (agency or department) on (date). Notification was delayed beyond the statutory ninety-day delay period pursuant to a determination by the court that such notice would seriously jeopardize an investigation concerning . You may have rights under the Right to Financial Privacy Act of 1978 [12 U.S.C. 3401 et. seq.]"

3407. Judicial subpoena

A Government authority may obtain financial records under section 3402(4) of this title pursuant to judicial subpoena only if—

(1) such subpoena is authorized by law and there is reason to believe that the records sought are relevant to a legitimate law enforcement inquiry;

(2) a copy of the subpoena has been served upon the customer or mailed to his last known address on or before the date on which the subpoena was served on the financial institution together with the following notice which shall state with reasonable specificity the nature of the law enforcement inquiry:

"Records or information concerning your transactions which are held by the financial institution named in the attached subpoena are being sought by this (agency or department or authority) in accordance with the Right to Financial Privacy Act of 1978 [12 U.S.C. 3401 et seq.] for the following purpose: If you desire that such records or information not be made available, you must:

"1.   Fill out the accompanying motion paper and sworn statement or write one of your own, stating that you are the customer whose records are being requested by the Government and either giving the reasons you believe that the records are not relevant to the legitimate law enforcement inquiry stated in this notice or any other legal basis for objecting to the release of the records.

"2.   File the motion and statement by mailing or delivering them to the clerk of the Court.

"3.   Serve the Government authority requesting the records by mailing or delivering a copy of your motion and statement to

"4.   Be prepared to come to court and present your position in further detail.

"5.   You do not need to have a lawyer, although you may wish to employ one to represent you and protect your rights.

"If you do not follow the above procedures, upon the expiration of ten days from the date of service or fourteen days from the date of mailing of this notice, the records or information requested therein will be made available. These records may be transferred to other government authorities for legitimate law enforcement inquiries, in which event you will be notified after the transfer;" and

(3) ten days have expired from the date of service or fourteen days from the date of mailing of the notice to the customer and within such time period the customer has not filed a sworn statement and motion to quash in an appropriate court, or the customer challenge provisions of section 3410 of this title have been complied with.

3408. Formal written request

A Government authority may request financial records under section 3402(5) of this title pursuant to a formal written request only if—

(1) no administrative summons or subpoena authority reasonably appears to be available to that Government authority to obtain financial records for the purpose for which such records are sought;

(2) the request is authorized by regulations promulgated by the head of the agency or department;

(3) there is reason to believe that the records sought are relevant to a legitimate law enforcement inquiry; and

(4)(A) a copy of the request has been served upon the customer or mailed to his last known address on or before the date on which the request was made to the financial institution together with the following notice which shall state with reasonable specificity the nature of the law enforcement inquiry:

"Records or information concerning your transactions held by the financial institution named in the attached request are being sought by this (agency or department) in accordance with the Right to Financial Privacy Act of 1978 [12 U.S.C. 3401 et seq.] for the following purpose:

"If you desire that such records or information not be made available, you must:

"1. Fill out the accompanying motion paper and sworn statement or write one of your own, stating that you are the customer whose records are being requested by the Government and either giving the reasons you believe that the records are not relevant to the legitimate law enforcement inquiry stated in this notice or any other legal basis for objecting to the release of the records.

"2.   File the motion and statement by mailing or delivering them to the Clerk of any one of the following United States District Courts:

"3.   Serve the Government authority requesting the records by mailing or delivering a copy of your motion and statement to

"4.   Be prepared to come to court and present your position in further detail.

"5.   You do not need to have a lawyer, although you may wish to employ one to represent you and protect your rights.

"If you do not follow the above procedures, upon the expiration of ten days after the date of service or fourteen days from the date of mailing of this notice, the records or information requested therein may be made available. These records may be transferred to other Government authorities for legitimate law enforcement inquiries, in which event you will be notified after the transfer;" and

(B)   ten days have expired from the date of service or fourteen days from the date of mailing of the notice by the customer and within such time period the customer has not filed a sworn statement and an application to enjoin the Government authority in an appropriate court, or the customer challenge provisions of section 3410 of this title have been complied with.

3409. Delayed notice

  (a) Application by Government authority; findings

Upon application of the Government authority, the customer notice required under section 3404(c), 3405(2), 3407(2), 3408(4), or 3412(b) of this title may be delayed by order of an appropriate court if the presiding judge or magistrate judge finds that—

    (1)   the investigation being conducted is within the lawful jurisdiction of the Government authority seeking the financial records;

    (2)   there is reason to believe that the records being sought are relevant to a legitimate law enforcement inquiry; and

    (3)   there is reason to believe that such notice will result in—

        (A)   endangering life or physical safety of any person;

        (B)   flight from prosecution;

        (C)   destruction of or tampering with evidence;

        (D)   intimidation of potential witnesses; or

        (E)   otherwise seriously jeopardizing an investigation or official proceeding or unduly delaying a trial or ongoing official proceeding to the same extent as the circumstances in the preceding subparagraphs.

An application for delay must be made with reasonable specificity.

  (b) Grant of delay order; duration and specifications; extensions; copy of request and notice to customer

    (1)   If the court makes the findings required in paragraphs (1), (2) and (3) of subsection (a) of this section, it shall enter an ex parte order granting the requested delay for a period not to exceed ninety days and an order prohibiting the financial institution from disclosing that records have been obtained or that a request for records has

been made, except that, if the records have been sought by a Government authority exercising financial controls over foreign accounts in the United States under section 5(b) of the Trading With the Enemy Act [12 U.S.C. 95a, 50 App. U.S.C. 5(b)], the International Economic Powers Act (title II, Public Law 95-223) [50 U.S.C. 1701 et seq.], or section 287c of title 22, and the court finds that there is reason to believe that such notice may endanger the lives or physical safety of a customer or group of customers, or any person or group of persons associated with a customer, the court may specify that the delay be indefinite.

(2) Extensions of the delay of notice provided in paragraph (1) of up to ninety days each may be granted by the court upon application, but only in accordance with this subsection.

(3) Upon expiration of the period of delay of notification under paragraph (1) or (2), the customer shall be served with or mailed a copy of the process or request together with the following notice which shall state with reasonable specificity the nature of the law enforcement inquiry: "Records or information concerning your transactions which are held by the financial institution named in the attached process or request were supplied to or requested by the Government authority named in the process or request on (date). Notification was withheld pursuant to a determination by the (title of court so ordering) under the Right to Financial Privacy Act of 1978 [12 U.S.C. 3401 et seq.] that such notice might (state reason). The purpose of the investigation or official proceeding was ."

(c) Notice requirement respecting emergency access to financial records

When access to financial records is obtained pursuant to section 3414(b) of this title (emergency access), the Government authority shall, unless a court has authorized delay of notice pursuant to subsections (a) and (b) of this section, as soon as practicable after such records are obtained serve upon the customer, or mail by registered or certified mail to his last known address, a copy of the request to the financial institution together with the following notice which shall state with reasonable specificity the nature of the law enforcement inquiry:

"Records concerning your transactions held by the financial institution named in the attached request were obtained by (agency or department) under the Right to Financial Privacy Act of 1978 [12 U.S.C. 3401 et seq.] on (date) for the following purpose:

"Emergency access to such records was obtained on the grounds that (state grounds)."

(d) Preservation of memorandums, affidavits, or other papers

Any memorandum, affidavit, or other paper filed in connection with a request for delay in notification shall be preserved by the court. Upon petition by the customer to whom such records pertain, the court may order disclosure of such papers to the petitioner unless the court makes the findings required in subsection (a) of this section.

3410. Customer challenges

(a) Filing of motion to quash or application to enjoin; proper court; contents

Within ten days of service or within fourteen days of mailing of a subpoena, summons, or formal written request, a customer may file a motion to quash an administrative summons or judicial subpoena, or an application to enjoin a Government authority from obtaining financial records pursuant to a formal written request, with copies served upon the Government authority. A motion to quash a judicial subpoena shall be filed in the court which issued the subpoena. A motion to quash an administrative summons or an application to enjoin a Government authority from obtaining records pursuant to a formal written request shall be filed in the appropriate United States district court. Such motion or application shall contain an affidavit or sworn statement—

(1)   stating that the applicant is a customer of the financial institution from which financial records pertaining to him have been sought; and

(2)   stating the applicant's reasons for believing that the financial records sought are not relevant to the legitimate law enforcement inquiry stated by the Government authority in its notice, or that there has not been substantial compliance with the provisions of this chapter.

Service shall be made under this section upon a Government authority by delivering or mailing by registered or certified mail a copy of the papers to the person, office, or department specified in the notice which the customer has received pursuant to this chapter. For the purposes of this section, "delivery" has the meaning stated in rule 5(b) of the Federal Rules of Civil Procedure.

(b) Filing of response; additional proceedings

If the court finds that the customer has complied with subsection (a) of this section, it shall order the Government authority to file a sworn response, which may be filed in camera if the Government includes in its response the reasons which make in camera review appropriate. If the court is unable to determine the motion or application on the basis of the parties' initial allegations and response, the court may conduct such additional proceedings as it deems appropriate. All such proceedings shall be completed and the motion or application decided within seven calendar days of the filing of the Government's response.

(c) Decision of court

If the court finds that the applicant is not the customer to whom the financial records sought by the Government authority pertain, or that there is a demonstrable reason to believe that the law enforcement inquiry is legitimate and a reasonable belief that the records sought are relevant to that inquiry, it shall deny the motion or application, and, in the case of an administrative summons or court order other than a search warrant, order such process enforced. If the court finds that the applicant is the customer to whom the records sought by the Government authority pertain, and that there is not a demonstrable reason to believe that the law enforcement inquiry is legitimate and a reasonable belief that the records sought are relevant to that inquiry, or that there has not been substantial compliance with the provisions of this chapter, it shall order the process quashed or enjoin the Government authority's formal written request.

(d) Appeals

A court ruling denying a motion or application under this section shall not be deemed a final order and no interlocutory appeal may be taken therefrom by the customer. An appeal of a ruling denying a motion or application made under this section may be taken by the customer

(1)   within such period of time as provided by law as part of any appeal from a final order in any legal proceeding

initiated against him arising out of or based upon the financial records, or

(2)   within thirty days after a notification that no legal pro-ceeding is contemplated against him. The Government authority obtaining the financial records shall promptly notify a customer when a determination has been made that no legal proceeding against him is contemplated. After one hundred and eighty days from the denial of the motion or application, if the Government authority obtaining the records has not initiated such a proceed-ing, a supervisory official of the Government authority shall certify to the appropriate court that no such deter-mination has been made. The court may require that such certifications be made, at reasonable intervals thereafter, until either notification to the customer has occurred or a legal proceeding is initiated as described in clause (A).

(e) Sole judicial remedy available to customer

The challenge procedures of this chapter constitute the sole judicial remedy available to a customer to oppose disclosure of financial records pursuant to this chapter.

(f) Affect on challenges by financial institutions

Nothing in this chapter shall enlarge or restrict any rights of a financial institution to challenge requests for records made by a Government authority under existing law. Nothing in this chapter shall entitle a customer to assert the rights of a financial institution.

3411. Duty of financial institutions

Upon receipt of a request for financial records made by a Government authority under section 3405 or 3407 of this title, the financial institution shall, unless otherwise provided by law, proceed to assemble the records requested and must be prepared to deliver the records to the Government authority upon receipt of the certificate required under section 3403(b) of this title.

3412. Use of information

(a) Transfer of financial records to other agencies or departments; certification

Financial records originally obtained pursuant to this chapter shall not be transferred to another agency or department unless the transferring agency or department certifies in writing that there is reason to believe that the records are relevant to a legitimate law enforcement inquiry within the jurisdiction of the receiving agency or department.

(b) Mailing of copy of certification and notice to customer

When financial records subject to this chapter are transferred pursuant to subsection (a) of this section, the transferring agency or department shall, within fourteen days, send to the customer a copy of the certification made pursuant to subsection (a) of this section and the following notice, which shall state the nature of the law enforcement inquiry with reasonable specificity:

"Copies of, or information contained in, your financial records lawfully in possession of have been furnished to pursuant to the Right to Financial Privacy Act of 1978 [12 U.S.C. 3401 et seq.] for the following purpose: . If you believe that this transfer has not been made to further a legitimate law enforcement inquiry, you may have legal rights under the Right to Financial Privacy Act of 1978 or the Privacy Act of 1974 [5 U.S.C. 552a]."

(c) Court-ordered delays in mailing

Notwithstanding subsection (b) of this section, notice to the customer may be delayed if the transferring agency or department has obtained a court order delaying notice pursuant to section 3409(a) and (b) of this title and that order is still in effect, or if the receiving agency or department obtains a court order authorizing a delay in notice pursuant to section 3409(a) and (b) of this title. Upon the expiration of any such period of delay, the transferring agency or department shall serve to the customer the notice specified in subsection (b) of this section and the agency or department that obtained the court order authorizing a delay in notice pursuant to section 3409(a) and (b) of this title shall serve to the customer the notice specified in section 3409(b) of this title.

(d) Exchanges of examination reports by supervisory agencies; transfer of financial records to defend customer action; withholding of information

Nothing in this chapter prohibits any supervisory agency from exchanging examination reports or other information with another supervisory agency. Nothing in this chapter prohibits the transfer of a customer's financial records needed by counsel for a Government authority to defend an action brought by the customer. Nothing in this chapter shall authorize the withholding of information by any officer or employee of a supervisory agency from a duly authorized committee or subcommittee of Congress.

(e) Federal Financial Institutions Examination Council supervisory agencies; Securities and Exchange Commission; authorization of exchange of financial records or other information

Notwithstanding section 3401(6) of this title or any other provision of this chapter, the exchange of financial records or other information with respect to a financial institution, holding company, or any subsidiary of a depository institution or holding company, among and between the five member supervisory agencies of the Federal Financial Institutions Examination Council and the Securities and Exchange Commission is permitted.

(f) Transfer to Attorney General or Secretary of the Treasury

    (1)   In general

Nothing in this chapter shall apply when financial records obtained by an agency or department of the United States are disclosed or transferred to the Attorney General or the Secretary of the Treasury upon the certification by a supervisory level official of the transferring agency or department that—

        (A)   there is reason to believe that the records may be relevant to a violation of Federal criminal law; and

        (B)   the records were obtained in the exercise of the agency's or department's supervisory or regulatory functions.

    (2)   Limitation on use

Records so transferred shall be used only for official investigative or prosecutive purposes, for civil actions under section 1833a of this title, or for forfeiture under sections 981 or 982 of title 18 by the Department of Justice and only for criminal investigative purposes relating to money laundering and other financial crimes by the Department of the Treasury and shall, upon completion of the investigation or prosecution (including any appeal), be returned only to the transferring agency or department. No agency or department so transferring such records shall be deemed to have waived any privilege applicable to those records under law.

3413. Exceptions

(a) Disclosure of financial records not identified with particular customers

Nothing in this chapter prohibits the disclosure of any financial records or information which is not identified with or identifiable as being derived from the financial records of a particular customer.

(b) Disclosure to, or examination by, supervisory agency pursuant to exercise of supervisory, regulatory, or monetary functions with respect to financial institutions, holding companies, subsidiaries, institution-affiliated parties, or other persons

This chapter shall not apply to the examination by or disclosure to any supervisory agency of financial records or information in the exercise of its supervisory, regulatory, or monetary functions, including conservatorship or receivership functions, with respect to any financial institution, holding company, subsidiary of a financial institution or holding company, institution-affiliated party (within the meaning of section 1813(u) of this title) with respect to a financial institution, holding company, or subsidiary, or other person participating in the conduct of the affairs thereof.

(c) Disclosure pursuant to title 26

Nothing in this chapter prohibits the disclosure of financial records in accordance with procedures authorized by title 26.

(d) Disclosure pursuant to Federal statute or rule promulgated thereunder

Nothing in this chapter shall authorize the withholding of financial records or information required to be reported in accordance with any Federal statute or rule promulgated thereunder.

(e) Disclosure pursuant to Federal Rules of Criminal Procedure or comparable rules of other courts

Nothing in this chapter shall apply when financial records are sought by a Government authority under the Federal Rules of Civil or Criminal Procedure or comparable rules of other courts in connection with litigation to which the Government authority and the customer are parties.

(f) Disclosure pursuant to administrative subpoena issued by administrative law judge

Nothing in this chapter shall apply when financial records are sought by a Government authority pursuant to an administrative subpoena issued by an administrative law judge in an adjudicatory proceeding subject to section 554 of title 5 and to which the Government authority and the customer are parties.

(g) Disclosure pursuant to legitimate law enforcement inquiry respecting name, address, account number, and type of account of particular customers

The notice requirements of this chapter and sections 3410 and 3412 of this title shall not apply when a Government authority by a means described in section 3402 of this title and for a legitimate law enforcement inquiry is seeking only the name, address, account number, and type of account of any customer or ascertainable group of customers associated (1) with a financial transaction or class of financial transactions, or (2) with a foreign country or subdivision thereof in the case of a Government authority exercising financial controls over foreign accounts in the United States under section 5(b) of the Trading With the Enemy Act [12 U.S.C. 95a, 50 App. U.S.C. 5(b)]; the International Emergency Economic Powers Act [title II, Public Law 95-223) [50 U.S.C. 1701 et seq.]; or section 287c of title 22.

(h) Disclosure pursuant to lawful proceeding, investigation, etc., directed at financial institution or legal entity or consideration or administration respecting Government loans, loan guarantees, etc.

(1) Nothing in this chapter (except sections 3403, 3417 and 3418 of this title) shall apply when financial records are sought by a Government authority—

(A)   in connection with a lawful proceeding, investigation, examination, or inspection directed at a financial institution (whether or not such proceeding, investigation, examination, or inspection is also directed at a customer) or at a legal entity which is not a customer; or

(B)   in connection with the authority's consideration or administration of assistance to the customer in the form of a Government loan, loan guaranty, or loan insurance program.

(2)   When financial records are sought pursuant to this subsection, the Government authority shall submit to the financial institution the certificate required by section 3403(b) of this title. For access pursuant to paragraph (1)(B), no further certification shall be required for subsequent access by the certifying Government authority during the term of the loan, loan guaranty, or loan insurance agreement.

(3)   After the effective date of this chapter, whenever a customer applies for participation in a Government loan, loan guaranty, or loan insurance program, the Government authority administering such program shall give the customer written notice of the authority's access rights under this subsection. No further notification shall be required for subsequent access by that authority during the term of the loan, loan guaranty, or loan insurance program.

(4)   Financial records obtained pursuant to this subsection may be used only for the purpose for which they were originally obtained, and may be transferred to another agency or department only when the transfer is to facili-

tate a lawful proceeding, investigation, examination, or inspection directed at a financial institution (whether or not such proceeding, investigation, examination, or inspection is also directed at a customer), or at a legal entity which is not a customer, except that—

(A) nothing in this paragraph prohibits the use or transfer of a customer's financial records needed by counsel representing a Government authority in a civil action arising from a Government loan, loan guaranty, or loan insurance program; and

(B) nothing in this paragraph prohibits a Government authority providing assistance to a customer in the form of a loan, loan guaranty, or loan insurance agreement from using or transferring financial records necessary to process, service or foreclose a loan, or to collect on an indebtedness to the Government resulting from a customer's default.

(5) Notification that financial records obtained pursuant to this subsection may relate to a potential civil, criminal, or regulatory violation by a customer may be given to an agency or department with jurisdiction over that violation, and such agency or department may then seek access to the records pursuant to the provisions of this chapter.

(6) Each financial institution shall keep a notation of each disclosure made pursuant to paragraph (1)(B) of this subsection, including the date of such disclosure and the Government authority to which it was made. The customer shall be entitled to inspect this information.

(i) Disclosure pursuant to issuance of subpoena or court order respecting grand jury proceedings

Nothing in this chapter (except sections 3415 and 3420 of this title) shall apply to any subpoena or court order issued in connection with proceedings before a grand jury, except that a court shall have authority to order a financial institution, on which a grand jury subpoena for customer records has been served, not to notify the customer of the existence of the subpoena or information that has been furnished to the grand jury, under circumstances and for the period specified and pursuant to the procedures established in section 3409 of this title.

(j) Disclosure pursuant to proceeding, investigation, etc., instituted by General Accounting Office and directed at a government authority

This chapter shall not apply when financial records are sought by the General Accounting Office pursuant to an authorized proceeding, investigation, examination or audit directed at a government authority.

(k) Disclosure necessary for proper administration of programs of withholding taxes on nonresident aliens, Federal Old-Age Survivors, and Disability Insurance Benefits, and Railroad Retirement Act Benefits

   (1) Nothing in this chapter shall apply to the disclosure by the financial institution of the name and address of any customer to the Department of the Treasury, the Social Security Administration, or the Railroad Retirement Board, where the disclosure of such information is necessary to, and such information is solely for the purpose of, the proper administration of section 1441 of title 26, title II of the Social Security Act [42 U.S.C. 401 et

seq.], or the Railroad Retirement Act of 1974 [45 U.S.C. 231 et seq.].

(2) Notwithstanding any other provision of law, any request authorized by paragraph (1) (and the information contained therein) may be used by the financial institution or its agents solely for the purpose of providing the customer's name and address to the Department of the Treasury, the Social Security Administration, or the Railroad Retirement Board and shall be barred from redisclosure by the financial institution or its agents.

(l) Crimes against financial institutions by insiders

Nothing in this chapter shall apply when any financial institution or supervisory agency provides any financial record of any officer, director, employee, or controlling shareholder (within the meaning of subparagraph (A) or (B) of section 1841(a)(2) of this title or subparagraph (A) or (B) of section 1730(a)(2) of this title) of such institution, or of any major borrower from such institution who there is reason to believe may be acting in concert with any such officer, director, employee, or controlling shareholder, to the Attorney General of the United States, to a State law enforcement agency, or, in the case of a possible violation of subchapter II of chapter 53 of title 31, to the Secretary of the Treasury if there is reason to believe that such record is relevant to a possible violation by such person of—

(1) any law relating to crimes against financial institutions or supervisory agencies by directors, officers, employees, or controlling shareholders of, or by borrowers from, financial institutions; or

(2) any provision of subchapter II of chapter 53 of title 31 or of section 1956 or 1957 of title 18.

No supervisory agency which transfers any such record under this subsection shall be deemed to have waived any privilege applicable to that record under law.

(m) Disclosure to, or examination by, employees or agents of Board of Governors of Federal Reserve System or Federal Reserve Bank

This chapter shall not apply to the examination by or disclosure to employees or agents of the Board of Governors of the Federal Reserve System or any Federal Reserve Bank of financial records or information in the exercise of the Federal Reserve System's authority to extend credit to the financial institutions or others.

(n) Disclosure to, or examination by, Resolution Trust Corporation or its employees or agents

This chapter shall not apply to the examination by or disclosure to the Resolution Trust Corporation or its employees or agents of financial records or information in the exercise of its conservatorship, receivership, or liquidation functions with respect to a financial institution.

(o) Disclosure to, or examination by, Federal Housing Finance Board or Federal home loan banks

This chapter shall not apply to the examination by or disclosure to the Federal Housing Finance Board or any of the Federal home loan banks of financial records or information in the exercise of the Federal Housing Finance Board's authority to extend credit (either directly or through a Federal home loan bank) to financial institutions or others.

(p) Access to information necessary for administration of certain veteran benefits laws

(1) Nothing in this chapter shall apply to the disclosure by the financial institution of the name and address of any customer to the Department of Veterans Affairs where the disclosure of such information is necessary to, and

such information is used solely for the purposes of, the proper administration of benefits programs under laws administered by the Secretary.

(2)   Notwithstanding any provision of law, any request authorized by paragraph (1) (and the information contained therein) may be used by the financial institution or its agents solely for the purpose of providing the customer's name and address to the Department of Veterans Affairs and shall be barred from redisclosure by the financial institution or its agents.

3414. Special procedures

(a)(1)   Nothing in this chapter (except sections 3415, 3417, 3418, and 3421 of this title) shall apply to the production and disclosure of financial records pursuant to requests from—

(A)   a Government authority authorized to conduct foreign counter—or foreign positive-intelligence activities for purposes of conducting such activities or;

(B)   the Secret Service for the purpose of conducting its protective functions [18 U.S.C. 3056; 3 U.S.C. 202, Public Law 90-331, as amended].

(2)   In the instances specified in paragraph (1), the Government authority shall submit to the financial institution the certificate required in section 3403(b) of this title signed by a supervisory official of a rank designated by the head of the Government authority.

(3)   No financial institution, or officer, employee, or agent of such institution, shall disclose to any person that a

Government authority described in paragraph (1) has sought or obtained access to a customer's financial records.

(4)   The Government authority specified in paragraph (1) shall compile an annual tabulation of the occasions in which this section was used.

(5)   (A)   Financial institutions, officers, employees, and agents thereof, shall comply with a request for a customer's or entity's financial records made pursuant to this subsection by the Federal Bureau of Investigation when the Director of the Federal Bureau of Investigation (or the Director's designee) certifies in writing to the financial institutions that such records are sought for foreign counterintelligence purposes and that there are specific and articulable facts giving reason to believe that the customer or entity whose records are sought is a foreign power or an agent of a foreign power as defined in section 1801 of title 50.

(B)   The Federal Bureau of Investigation may disseminate information obtained pursuant to this paragraph only as provided in guidelines approved by the Attorney General for foreign intelligence collection and foreign counterintelligence investigations conducted by the Federal Bureau of Investigation, and with respect to dissemination to an agency of the United States, only if such information is clearly relevant to the authorized responsibilities of such agency.

(C)   On a semiannual basis the Attorney General shall fully inform the Permanent Select

Committee on Intelligence of the House of Representatives and the Select Committee on Intelligence of the Senate concerning all requests made pursuant to this paragraph.

(D)   No financial institution, or officer, employee, or agent of such institution, shall disclose to any person that the Federal Bureau of Investigation has sought or obtained access to a customer's or entity's financial records under this paragraph.

(b)(1)   Nothing in this chapter shall prohibit a Government authority from obtaining financial records from a financial institution if the Government authority determines that delay in obtaining access to such records would create imminent danger of—

(A)   physical injury to any person;

(B)   serious property damage; or

(C)   flight to avoid prosecution.

(2)   In the instances specified in paragraph (1), the Government shall submit to the financial institution the certificate required in section 3403(b) of this title signed by a supervisory official of a rank designated by the head of the Government authority.

(3)   Within five days of obtaining access to financial records under this subsection, the Government authority shall file with the appropriate court a signed, sworn statement of a supervisory official of a rank designated by the head of the Government authority setting forth the grounds for the emergency access. The Government authority shall thereafter comply with the notice provisions of section 3409(c) of this title.

(4)   The Government authority specified in paragraph (1) shall compile an annual tabluation of the occasions in which this section was used.

3415. Cost reimbursement

Except for records obtained pursuant to section 3403(d) or 3413(a) through (h) of this title, or as otherwise provided by law, a Government authority shall pay to the financial institution assembling or providing financial records pertaining to a customer and in accordance with procedures established by this chapter a fee for reimbursement for such costs as are reasonably necessary and which have been directly incurred in searching for, reproducing, or transporting books, papers, records, or other data required or requested to be produced. The Board of Governors of the Federal Reserve System shall, by regulation, establish the rates and conditions under which such payment may be made.

3416. Jurisdiction

An action to enforce any provision of this chapter may be brought in any appropriate United States district court without regard to the amount in controversy within three years from the date on which the violation occurs or the date of discovery of such violation, whichever is later.

3417. Civil penalties

(a) Liability of agencies or departments of United States of financial institutions

Any agency or department of the United States or financial institution obtaining or disclosing financial records or information contained therein in violation of this chapter is liable to the customer to whom such records relate in an amount equal to the sum of—

(1) $100 without regard to the volume of records involved;

(2) any actual damages sustained by the customer as a result of the disclosure;

(3) such punitive damages as the court may allow, where the violation is found to have been willful or intentional; and

(4) in the case of any successful action to enforce liability under this section, the costs of the action together with reasonable attorney's fees as determined by the court.

(b) Disciplinary action for willful or intentional violation of chapter by agents or employees of department or agency

Whenever the court determines that any agency or department of the United States has violated any provision of this chapter and the court finds that the circumstances surrounding the violation raise questions of whether an officer or employee of the department or agency acted willfully or intentionally with respect to the violation, the Director of the Office of Personnel Management shall promptly initiate a proceeding to determine whether disciplinary action is warranted against the agent or employee who was primarily responsible for the violation. The Director, after investigation and consideration of the evidence submitted, shall submit his findings and recommendations to the administrative authority of the agency concerned and shall send copies of the findings and recommendations to the officer or employee or his representative. The administrative authority shall take the corrective action that the Director recommends.

(c) Good faith defense

Any financial institution or agent or employee thereof making a disclosure of financial records pursuant to this chapter in good-faith reliance upon a certificate by any Government authority or pursuant to the provisions of section 3413(1) of this title shall not be liable to the customer for such disclosure under this chapter, the constitution of any State, or any law or regulation of any State or political subdivision of any State.

(d) Exclusive judicial remedies and sanctions

The remedies and sanctions described in this chapter shall be the only authorized judicial remedies and sanctions for violations of this chapter.

3418. Injunctive relief

In addition to any other remedy contained in this chapter, injunctive relief shall be available to require that the procedures of this chapter are complied with. In the event of any successful action, costs together with reasonable attorney's fees as determined by the court may be recovered.

3419. Suspension of limitations

If any individual files a motion or application under this chapter which has the effect of delaying the access of a Government authority to financial records pertaining to such individual, any applicable statute of limitations shall be deemed to be tolled for the period extending from the date such motion or application was filed until the date upon which the motion or application is decided.

3420. Grand jury information; notification of certain persons prohibited

(a) Financial records about a customer obtained from a financial institution pursuant to a subpoena issued under the authority of a Federal grand jury—

    (1) shall be returned and actually presented to the grand jury unless the volume of such records makes such return and actual presentation impractical in which case the grand jury shall be provided with a description of the contents of the records;

    (2) hall be used only for the purpose of considering whether to issue an indictment or presentment by that grand

jury, or of prosecuting a crime for which that indictment or presentment is issued, or for a purpose authorized by rule 6(e) of the Federal Rules of Criminal Procedure;

(3)   shall be destroyed or returned to the financial institution if not used for one of the purposes specified in paragraph (2); and

(4)   shall not be maintained, or a description of the contents of such records shall not be maintained, by any Government authority other than in the sealed records of the grand jury, unless such records has been used in the prosecution of a crime for which the grand jury issued an indictment or presentment or for a purpose authorized by rule 6(e) of the Federal Rules of Criminal Procedure.

(b)(1)   No officer, director, partner, employee, or shareholder of, or agent or attorney for, a financial institution shall, directly or indirectly, notify any person named in a grand jury subpoena served on such institution in connection with an investigation relating to a possible—

(A)   crime against any financial institution or supervisory agency or crime involving a violation of the Controlled Substance Act [21 U.S.C. 801 et seq.], the Controlled Substances Import and Export Act [21 U.S.C. 951 et seq.], section 1956 or 1957 of title 18, sections 5313, 5316, and 5324 of title 31, or section 6050I of title 26; or

(B)   conspiracy to commit such a crime, about the existence or contents of such subpoena, or information that has been furnished to the grand jury in response to such subpoena.

(2)   Section 1818 of this title and section 1786(k)(2) of this title shall apply to any violation of this subsection.

3421. Repealed

3422. Applicability to Securities and Exchange Commission

Except as provided in the Securities and Exchange Act of 1934 [15 U.S.C. 78a et seq.], this chapter shall apply with respect to the Securities and Exchange Commission.

Appendix J—Fair Credit Reporting Act (FCRA)

As a public service, the staff of the Federal Trade Commission (FTC) has prepared the following complete text of the Fair Credit Reporting Act (FCRA), 15 U.S.C. § 1681 et seq. Although staff generally followed the format of the U.S. Code as published by the Government Printing Office, the format of this text does differ in minor ways from the Code (and from West's U.S. Code Annotated). For example, this version uses FCRA section numbers (§§ 601-625) in the headings. (The relevant U.S. Code citation is included with each section heading and each reference to the FCRA in the text.)

This version of the FCRA is complete as of July 1999. It includes the amendments to the FCRA set forth in the Consumer Credit Reporting Reform Act of 1996 (Public Law 104-208, the Omnibus Consolidated Appropriations Act for Fiscal Year 1997, Title II, Subtitle D, Chapter 1), Section 311 of the Intelligence Authorization for Fiscal Year 1998 (Public Law 105-107), and the Consumer Reporting Employment Clarification Act of 1998 (Public Law 105-347).

Table of Contents

§ 607 Compliance procedures

§ 608 Disclosures to governmental agencies

§ 609 Disclosures to consumers

§ 610 Conditions and form of disclosure to consumers

§ 611 Procedure in case of disputed accuracy

§ 612 Charges for certain disclosures

§ 613 Public record information for employment purposes

§ 614 Restrictions on investigative consumer reports

§ 615 Requirements on users of consumer reports

§ 616 Civil liability for willful noncompliance

§ 617 Civil liability for negligent noncompliance

§ 618 Jurisdiction of courts; limitation of actions

§ 619 Obtaining information under false pretenses

§ 620 Unauthorized disclosures by officers or employees

§ 621 Administrative enforcement

§ 622 Information on overdue child support obligations

§ 623 Responsibilities of furnishers of
information to consumer reporting agencies

§ 624 Relation to State laws

§ 625 Disclosures to FBI for counterintelligence purposes

*   *   *

§ 601. Short title

This title may be cited as the Fair Credit Reporting Act.

§ 602. Congressional findings and statement of purpose [15 U.S.C. § 1681]

(a) Accuracy and fairness of credit reporting. The Congress makes the following findings:

    (1) The banking system is dependent upon fair and accurate credit reporting. Inaccurate credit reports directly

impair the efficiency of the banking system, and unfair credit reporting methods undermine the public confidence which is essential to the continued functioning of the banking system.

(2) An elaborate mechanism has been developed for investigating and evaluating the credit worthiness, credit standing, credit capacity, character, and general reputation of consumers.

(3) Consumer reporting agencies have assumed a vital role in assembling and evaluating consumer credit and other information on consumers.

(4) There is a need to insure that consumer reporting agencies exercise their grave responsibilities with fairness, impartiality, and a respect for the consumer's right to privacy.

(b) Reasonable procedures. It is the purpose of this title to require that consumer reporting agencies adopt reasonable procedures for meeting the needs of commerce for consumer credit, personnel, insurance, and other information in a manner which is fair and equitable to the consumer, with regard to the confidentiality, accuracy, relevancy, and proper utilization of such information in accordance with the requirements of this title.

§ 603. Definitions; rules of construction [15 U.S.C. § 1681a]

(a) Definitions and rules of construction set forth in this section are applicable for the purposes of this title.

(b) The term "person" means any individual, partnership, corporation, trust, estate, cooperative, association, government or governmental subdivision or agency, or other entity.

(c) The term "consumer" means an individual.

(d) Consumer report.

(1)   In general. The term "consumer report" means any written, oral, or other communication of any information by
a consumer reporting agency bearing on a consumer's
credit worthiness, credit standing, credit capacity, character, general reputation, personal characteristics, or
mode of living which is used or expected to be used or
collected in whole or in part for the purpose of serving
as a factor in establishing the consumer's eligibility for

    (A)   credit or insurance to be used primarily for per-
sonal, family, or household purposes;

    (B)   employment purposes; or

    (C)   any other purpose authorized under section 604
[§ 1681b].

(2)   Exclusions. The term "consumer report" does not include

    (A)   any

        (i)   report containing information solely as
to transactions or experiences between
the consumer and the person making
the report;

        (ii)   communication of that information
among persons related by common
ownership or affiliated by corporate
control; or

        (iii)   communication of other information
among persons related by common ownership or affiliated by corporate control, if
it is clearly and conspicuously disclosed to
the consumer that the information may be
communicated among such persons and
the consumer is given the opportunity,
before the time that the information is

initially communicated, to direct that such information not be communicated among such persons;

(B)   any authorization or approval of a specific extension of credit directly or indirectly by the issuer of a credit card or similar device;

(C)   any report in which a person who has been requested by a third party to make a specific extension of credit directly or indirectly to a consumer conveys his or her decision with respect to such request, if the third party advises the consumer of the name and address of the person to whom the request was made, and such person makes the disclosures to the consumer required under section 615 [§ 1681m]; or

(D)   a communication described in subsection (o).

(e) The term "investigative consumer report" means a consumer report or portion thereof in which information on a consumer's character, general reputation, personal characteristics, or mode of living is obtained through personal interviews with neighbors, friends, or associates of the consumer reported on or with others with whom he is acquainted or who may have knowledge concerning any such items of information. However, such information shall not include specific factual information on a consumer's credit record obtained directly from a creditor of the consumer or from a consumer reporting agency when such information was obtained directly from a creditor of the consumer or from the consumer.

(f) The term "consumer reporting agency" means any person which, for monetary fees, dues, or on a cooperative nonprofit basis, regularly engages in whole or in part in the practice of assembling or evaluating consumer credit information or other information on consumers for the purpose of furnishing consumer reports to third parties, and which uses any means or facility of interstate commerce for the purpose of preparing or furnishing consumer reports.

(g) The term "file," when used in connection with information on any consumer, means all of the information on that consumer recorded and retained by a consumer reporting agency regardless of how the information is stored.

(h) The term "employment purposes" when used in connection with a consumer report means a report used for the purpose of evaluating a consumer for employment, promotion, reassignment or retention as an employee.

(i) The term "medical information" means information or records obtained, with the consent of the individual to whom it relates, from licensed physicians or medical practitioners, hospitals, clinics, or other medical or medically related facilities.

(j) Definitions relating to child support obligations.

(1) Overdue support. The term "overdue support" has the meaning given to such term in section 666(e) of title 42 [Social Security Act, 42 U.S.C. § 666(e)].

(2) State or local child support enforcement agency. The term "State or local child support enforcement agency" means a State or local agency which administers a State or local program for establishing and enforcing child support obligations.

(k) Adverse action.

(1) Actions included. The term "adverse action"

(A) has the same meaning as in section 701(d)(6) of the Equal Credit Opportunity Act; and

(B) means

(i) a denial or cancellation of, an increase in any charge for, or a reduction or other adverse or unfavorable change in the terms of coverage or amount of, any insurance, existing or applied for, in connection with the underwriting of insurance;

(ii) a denial of employment or any other decision for employment purposes that adversely affects any current or prospective employee;

(iii) a denial or cancellation of, an increase in any charge for, or any other adverse or unfavorable change in the terms of, any license or benefit described in section 604(a)(3)(D) [§ 1681b]; and

(iv) an action taken or determination that is

(I) made in connection with an application that was made by, or a transaction that was initiated by, any consumer, or in connection with a review of an account under section 604(a)(3)(F)(ii)[§ 1681b]; and

(II) adverse to the interests of the consumer.

(2) Applicable findings, decisions, commentary, and orders. For purposes of any determination of whether an action is an adverse action under paragraph (1)(A), all appropriate final findings, decisions, commentary, and orders issued under section 701(d)(6) of the Equal Credit

Opportunity Act by the Board of Governors of the Federal Reserve System or any court shall apply.

(l) Firm offer of credit or insurance. The term "firm offer of credit or insurance" means any offer of credit or insurance to a consumer that will be honored if the consumer is determined, based on information in a consumer report on the consumer, to meet the specific criteria used to select the consumer for the offer, except that the offer may be further conditioned on one or more of the following:

(1)   The consumer being determined, based on information in the consumer's application for the credit or insurance, to meet specific criteria bearing on credit worthiness or insurability, as applicable, that are established

(A)   before selection of the consumer for the offer; and

(B)   for the purpose of determining whether to extend credit or insurance pursuant to the offer.

(2)   Verification

(A)   that the consumer continues to meet the specific criteria used to select the consumer for the offer, by using information in a consumer report on the consumer, information in the consumer's application for the credit or insurance, or other information bearing on the credit worthiness or insurability of the consumer; or

(B)   of the information in the consumer's application for the credit or insurance, to determine that the consumer meets the specific criteria bearing on credit worthiness or insurability.

(3)   The consumer furnishing any collateral that is a requirement for the extension of the credit or insurance that was

    (A)   established before selection of the consumer for the offer of credit or insurance; and

    (B)   disclosed to the consumer in the offer of credit or insurance.

(m) Credit or insurance transaction that is not initiated by the consumer.

The term "credit or insurance transaction that is not initiated by the consumer" does not include the use of a consumer report by a person with which the consumer has an account or insurance policy, for purposes of

(1)   reviewing the account or insurance policy; or

(2)   collecting the account.

(n) State. The term "State" means any State, the Commonwealth of Puerto Rico, the District of Columbia, and any territory or possession of the United States.

(o) Excluded communications. A communication is described in this subsection if it is a communication

(1)   that, but for subsection (d)(2)(D), would be an investigative consumer report;

(2)   that is made to a prospective employer for the purpose of

    (A)   procuring an employee for the employer; or

    (B)   procuring an opportunity for a natural person to work for the employer;

(3)   that is made by a person who regularly performs such procurement;

(4)   that is not used by any person for any purpose other than a purpose described in subparagraph (A) or (B) of paragraph (2); and

(5)   with respect to which

(A) the consumer who is the subject of the communication

    (i)   consents orally or in writing to the nature and scope of the communication, before the collection of any information for the purpose of making the communication;

    (ii)   consents orally or in writing to the making of the communication to a prospective employer, before the making of the communication; and

    (iii)   in the case of consent under clause (i) or (ii) given orally, is provided written confirmation of that consent by the person making the communication, not later than 3 business days after the receipt of the consent by that person;

(B)   the person who makes the communication does not, for the purpose of making the communication, make any inquiry that if made by a prospective employer of the consumer who is the subject of the communication would violate any applicable Federal or State equal employment opportunity law or regulation; and

(C)   the person who makes the communication

    (i)   discloses in writing to the consumer who is the subject of the communication, not later than 5 business days after receiving any request from the consumer for such disclosure, the nature and substance of all information in the consumer's file at the time of the request, except that the sources of any information that is acquired solely for use in making the communication and is actually used for no other purpose, need not be disclosed other than under appropriate discovery procedures in any court of competent jurisdiction in which an action is brought; and

(ii) notifies the consumer who is the subject of the communication, in writing, of the consumer's right to request the information described in clause (i).

(p) Consumer reporting agency that compiles and maintains files on consumers on a nationwide basis. The term "consumer reporting agency that compiles and maintains files on consumers on a nationwide basis" means a consumer reporting agency that regularly engages in the practice of assembling or evaluating, and maintaining, for the purpose of furnishing consumer reports to third parties bearing on a consumer's credit worthiness, credit standing, or credit capacity, each of the following regarding consumers residing nationwide:

(1) Public record information.

(2) Credit account information from persons who furnish that information regularly and in the ordinary course of business.

§ 604. Permissible purposes of consumer reports [15 U.S.C. § 1681b]

(a) In general. Subject to subsection (c), any consumer reporting agency may furnish a consumer report under the following circumstances and no other:

(1)   In response to the order of a court having jurisdiction to issue such an order, or a subpoena issued in connection with proceedings before a Federal grand jury.

(2)   In accordance with the written instructions of the consumer to whom it relates.

(3)   To a person which it has reason to believe

    (A)   intends to use the information in connection with a credit transaction involving the consumer on whom the information is to be furnished and involving the extension of credit to, or review or collection of an account of, the consumer; or

    (B)   intends to use the information for employment purposes; or

    (C)   intends to use the information in connection with the underwriting of insurance involving the consumer; or

    (D)   intends to use the information in connection with a determination of the consumer's eligibility for a license or other benefit granted by a governmental instrumentality required by law to consider an applicant's financial responsibility or status; or

    (E)   intends to use the information, as a potential investor or servicer, or current insurer, in connection with a valuation of, or an assessment of the credit or prepayment risks associated with, an existing credit obligation; or

     (F)   otherwise has a legitimate business need for the information

          (i)   in connection with a business transaction that is initiated by the consumer; or

          (ii)   to review an account to determine whether the consumer continues to meet the terms of the account.

(4)   In response to a request by the head of a State or local child support enforcement agency (or a State or local government official authorized by the head of such an agency), if the person making the request certifies to the consumer reporting agency that

     (A)   the consumer report is needed for the purpose of establishing an individual's capacity to make child support payments or determining the appropriate level of such payments;

     (B)   the paternity of the consumer for the child to which the obligation relates has been established or acknowledged by the consumer in accordance with State laws under which the obligation arises (if required by those laws);

     (C)   the person has provided at least 10 days' prior notice to the consumer whose report is requested, by certified or registered mail to the last known address of the consumer, that the report will be requested; and

     (D)   the consumer report will be kept confidential, will be used solely for a purpose described in subparagraph (A), and will not be used in connection with any other civil, administrative, or criminal proceeding, or for any other purpose.

(5) To an agency administering a State plan under Section 454 of the Social Security Act (42 U.S.C. § 654) for use to set an initial or modified child support award.

(b) Conditions for furnishing and using consumer reports for employment purposes.

(1) Certification from user. A consumer reporting agency may furnish a consumer report for employment purposes only if

(A) the person who obtains such report from the agency certifies to the agency that

(i) the person has complied with paragraph (2) with respect to the consumer report, and the person will comply with paragraph (3) with respect to the consumer report if paragraph (3) becomes applicable; and

(ii) information from the consumer report will not be used in violation of any applicable Federal or State equal employment opportunity law or regulation; and

(B) the consumer reporting agency provides with the report, or has previously provided, a summary of the consumer's rights under this title, as prescribed by the Federal Trade Commission under section 609(c)(3) [§ 1681g].

(2) Disclosure to consumer.

(A) In general. Except as provided in subparagraph (B), a person may not procure a consumer report, or cause a consumer report to be procured, for employment purposes with respect to any consumer, unless—

       (i)   a clear and conspicuous disclosure has been made in writing to the consumer at any time before the report is procured or caused to be procured, in a document that consists solely of the disclosure, that a consumer report may be obtained for employment purposes; and

       (ii)   the consumer has authorized in writing (which authorization may be made on the document referred to in clause (i)) the procurement of the report by that person.

(B)   Application by mail, telephone, computer, or other similar means. If a consumer described in subparagraph (C) applies for employment by mail, telephone, computer, or other similar means, at any time before a consumer report is procured or caused to be procured in connection with that application—

       (i)   the person who procures the consumer report on the consumer for employment purposes shall provide to the consumer, by oral, written, or electronic means, notice that a consumer report may be obtained for employment purposes, and a summary of the consumer's rights under section 615(a)(3); and

       (ii)   the consumer shall have consented, orally, in writing, or electronically to the procurement of the report by that person.

(C)   Scope. Subparagraph (B) shall apply to a person procuring a consumer report on a consumer in connection with the consumer's application for employment only if—

(i) the consumer is applying for a position over which the Secretary of Transportation has the power to establish qualifications and maximum hours of service pursuant to the provisions of section 31502 of title 49, or a position subject to safety regulation by a State transportation agency; and

(ii) as of the time at which the person procures the report or causes the report to be procured the only interaction between the consumer and the person in connection with that employment application has been by mail, telephone, computer, or other similar means.

(3) Conditions on use for adverse actions.

  (A) In general. Except as provided in subparagraph (B), in using a consumer report for employment purposes, before taking any adverse action based in whole or in part on the report, the person intending to take such adverse action shall provide to the consumer to whom the report relates—

    (i) a copy of the report; and

    (ii) a description in writing of the rights of the consumer under this title, as prescribed by the Federal Trade Commission under section 609(c)(3).

  (B) Application by mail, telephone, computer, or other similar means.

(i)   If a consumer described in subparagraph (C) applies for employment by mail, telephone, computer, or other similar means, and if a person who has procured a consumer report on the consumer for employment purposes takes adverse action on the employment application based in whole or in part on the report, then the person must provide to the consumer to whom the report relates, in lieu of the notices required under subparagraph (A) of this section and under section 615(a), within 3 business days of taking such action, an oral, written or electronic notification—

(I)   that adverse action has been taken based in whole or in part on a consumer report received from a consumer reporting agency;

(II)   of the name, address and telephone number of the consumer reporting agency that furnished the consumer report (including a toll-free telephone number established by the agency if the agency compiles and maintains files on consumers on a nationwide basis);

(III)   that the consumer reporting agency did not make the decision to take the adverse action and is unable to provide to the consumer the specific reasons why the adverse action was taken; and

(IV)　that the consumer may, upon providing proper identification, request a free copy of a report and may dispute with the consumer reporting agency the accuracy or completeness of any information in a report.

(ii)　If, under clause (B)(i)(IV), the consumer requests a copy of a consumer report from the person who procured the report, then, within 3 business days of receiving the consumer's request, together with proper identification, the person must send or provide to the consumer a copy of a report and a copy of the consumer's rights as prescribed by the Federal Trade Commission under section 609(c)(3).

(C)　Scope. Subparagraph (B) shall apply to a person procuring a consumer report on a consumer in connection with the consumer's application for employment only if—

(i)　the consumer is applying for a position over which the Secretary of Transportation has the power to establish qualifications and maximum hours of service pursuant to the provisions of section 31502 of title

49, or a position subject to safety regulation by a State transportation agency; and

(ii) as of the time at which the person procures the report or causes the report to be procured the only interaction between the consumer and the person in connection with that employment application has been by mail, telephone, computer, or other similar means.

(4) Exception for national security investigations.

(A) In general. In the case of an agency or department of the United States Government which seeks to obtain and use a consumer report for employment purposes, paragraph (3) shall not apply to any adverse action by such agency or department which is based in part on such consumer report, if the head of such agency or department makes a written finding that—

(i) the consumer report is relevant to a national security investigation of such agency or department;

(ii) the investigation is within the jurisdiction of such agency or department;

(iii) there is reason to believe that compliance with paragraph (3) will—

(I) endanger the life or physical safety of any person;

(II) result in flight from prosecution;

(III) result in the destruction of, or tampering with, evidence relevant to the investigation;

(IV)   result in the intimidation of a potential witness relevant to the investigation;

(V)   result in the compromise of classified information; or

(VI)   otherwise seriously jeopardize or unduly delay the investigation or another official proceeding.

(B)   Notification of consumer upon conclusion of investigation. Upon the conclusion of a national security investigation described in subparagraph (A), or upon the determination that the exception under subparagraph (A) is no longer required for the reasons set forth in such subparagraph, the official exercising the authority in such subparagraph shall provide to the consumer who is the subject of the consumer report with regard to which such finding was made—

(i)   a copy of such consumer report with any classified information redacted as necessary;

(ii)   notice of any adverse action which is based, in part, on the consumer report; and

(iii)   the identification with reasonable specificity of the nature of the investigation for which the consumer report was sought.

(C)   Delegation by head of agency or department. For purposes of subparagraphs (A) and (B), the head of any agency or department of the United States Government may delegate his or her authorities under this paragraph to an official of such agency or department who has personnel security responsibilities and is a member of the Senior Executive Service or equivalent civilian or military rank.

(D) Report to the congress. Not later than January 31 of each year, the head of each agency and department of the United States Government that exercised authority under this paragraph during the preceding year shall submit a report to the Congress on the number of times the department or agency exercised such authority during the year.

(E) Definitions. For purposes of this paragraph, the following definitions shall apply:

(i) Classified information. The term 'classified information' means information that is protected from unauthorized disclosure under Executive Order No. 12958 or successor orders.

(ii) National security investigation. The term 'national security investigation' means any official inquiry by an agency or department of the United States Government to determine the eligibility of a consumer to receive access or continued access to classified information or to determine whether classified information has been lost or compromised.

(c) Furnishing reports in connection with credit or insurance transactions that are not initiated by the consumer.

(1) In general. A consumer reporting agency may furnish a consumer report relating to any consumer pursuant to

subparagraph (A) or (C) of subsection (a)(3) in connection with any credit or insurance transaction that is not initiated by the consumer only if

(A)   the consumer authorizes the agency to provide such report to such person; or

(B)   (i)   the transaction consists of a firm offer of credit or insurance;

            (ii)   the consumer reporting agency has complied with subsection (e); and

            (iii)   there is not in effect an election by the consumer, made in accordance with subsection (e), to have the consumer's name and address excluded from lists of names provided by the agency pursuant to this paragraph.

(2)   Limits on information received under paragraph (1)(B). A person may receive pursuant to paragraph (1)(B) only

(A)   the name and address of a consumer;

(B)   an identifier that is not unique to the consumer and that is used by the person solely for the purpose of verifying the identity of the consumer; and

(C)   other information pertaining to a consumer that does not identify the relationship or experience of the consumer with respect to a particular creditor or other entity.

(3)   Information regarding inquiries. Except as provided in section 609(a)(5) [§ 1681g], a consumer reporting agency shall not furnish to any person a record of inquiries in connection with a credit or insurance transaction that is not initiated by a consumer.

(d) Reserved.

(e) Election of consumer to be excluded from lists.

> (1) In general. A consumer may elect to have the consumer's name and address excluded from any list provided by a consumer reporting agency under subsection (c)(1)(B) in connection with a credit or insurance transaction that is not initiated by the consumer, by notifying the agency in accordance with paragraph (2) that the consumer does not consent to any use of a consumer report relating to the consumer in connection with any credit or insurance transaction that is not initiated by the consumer.
>
> (2) Manner of notification. A consumer shall notify a consumer reporting agency under paragraph (1)
>
> > (A) through the notification system maintained by the agency under paragraph (5); or
> >
> > (B) by submitting to the agency a signed notice of election form issued by the agency for purposes of this subparagraph.
>
> (3) Response of agency after notification through system. Upon receipt of notification of the election of a consumer under paragraph (1) through the notification system maintained by the agency under paragraph (5), a consumer reporting agency shall
>
> > (A) inform the consumer that the election is effective only for the 2-year period following the election if the consumer does not submit to the agency a signed notice of election form issued by the agency for purposes of paragraph (2)(B); and
> >
> > (B) provide to the consumer a notice of election form, if requested by the consumer, not later than 5 business days after receipt of the notification of

the election through the system established under paragraph (5), in the case of a request made at the time the consumer provides notification through the system.

(4)   Effectiveness of election. An election of a consumer under paragraph (1)

(A)   shall be effective with respect to a consumer reporting agency beginning 5 business days after the date on which the consumer notifies the agency in accordance with paragraph (2);

(B)   shall be effective with respect to a consumer reporting agency

(i)   subject to subparagraph (C), during the 2-year period beginning 5 business days after the date on which the consumer notifies the agency of the election, in the case of an election for which a consumer notifies the agency only in accordance with paragraph (2)(A); or

(ii)   until the consumer notifies the agency under subparagraph (C), in the case of an election for which a consumer notifies the agency in accordance with paragraph (2)(B);

(C)   shall not be effective after the date on which the consumer notifies the agency, through the notification system established by the agency under paragraph (5), that the election is no longer effective; and

(D)   shall be effective with respect to each affiliate of the agency.

(5) Notification system.

    (A) In general. Each consumer reporting agency that, under subsection (c)(1)(B), furnishes a consumer report in connection with a credit or insurance transaction that is not initiated by a consumer, shall

        (i) establish and maintain a notification system, including a toll-free telephone number, which permits any consumer whose consumer report is maintained by the agency to notify the agency, with appropriate identification, of the consumer's election to have the consumer's name and address excluded from any such list of names and addresses provided by the agency for such a transaction; and

        (ii) publish by not later than 365 days after the date of enactment of the Consumer Credit Reporting Reform Act of 1996, and not less than annually thereafter, in a publication of general circulation in the area served by the agency

            (I) a notification that information in consumer files maintained by the agency may be used in connection with such transactions; and

            (II) the address and toll-free telephone number for consumers to use to notify the agency of the consumer's election under clause (I).

(B) Establishment and maintenance as compliance. Establishment and maintenance of a notification system (including a toll-free telephone number) and publication by a consumer reporting agency on the agency's own behalf and on behalf of any of its affiliates in accordance with this paragraph is deemed to be compliance with this paragraph by each of those affiliates.

(6) Notification system by agencies that operate nationwide. Each consumer reporting agency that compiles and maintains files on consumers on a nationwide basis shall establish and maintain a notification system for purposes of paragraph (5) jointly with other such consumer reporting agencies.

(f) Certain use or obtaining of information prohibited. A person shall not use or obtain a consumer report for any purpose unless

(1) the consumer report is obtained for a purpose for which the consumer report is authorized to be furnished under this section; and

(2) the purpose is certified in accordance with section 607 [§ 1681e] by a prospective user of the report through a general or specific certification.

(g) Furnishing reports containing medical information. A consumer reporting agency shall not furnish for employment purposes, or in connection with a credit or insurance transaction, a consumer report that contains medical information about a consumer, unless the consumer consents to the furnishing of the report.

§ 605. Requirements relating to information contained in consumer reports [15 U.S.C. § 1681c]

(a) Information excluded from consumer reports. Except as authorized under subsection (b) of this section, no consumer reporting agency may make any consumer report containing any of the following items of information:

(1)   Cases under title 11 [United States Code] or under the Bankruptcy Act that, from the date of entry of the order for relief or the date of adjudication, as the case may be, antedate the report by more than 10 years.

(2)   Civil suits, civil judgments, and records of arrest that from date of entry, antedate the report by more than seven years or until the governing statute of limitations has expired, whichever is the longer period.

(3)   Paid tax liens which, from date of payment, antedate the report by more than seven years.

(4)   Accounts placed for collection or charged to profit and loss which antedate the report by more than seven years.(1)

(5)   Any other adverse item of information, other than records of convictions of crimes which antedates the report by more than seven years.1

(b) Exempted cases. The provisions of subsection (a) of this section are not applicable in the case of any consumer credit report to be used in connection with

(1)   a credit transaction involving, or which may reasonably be expected to involve, a principal amount of $150,000 or more;

(2)   the underwriting of life insurance involving, or which may reasonably be expected to involve, a face amount of $150,000 or more; or

(3)   the employment of any individual at an annual salary which equals, or which may reasonably be expected to equal $75,000, or more.

(c) Running of reporting period.

   (1)   In general. The 7-year period referred to in paragraphs (4) and (6) ** of subsection (a) shall begin, with respect to any delinquent account that is placed for collection (internally or by referral to a third party, whichever is earlier), charged to profit and loss, or subjected to any similar action, upon the expiration of the 180-day period beginning on the date of the commencement of the delinquency which immediately preceded the collection activity, charge to profit and loss, or similar action.

   (2)   Effective date. Paragraph (1) shall apply only to items of information added to the file of a consumer on or after the date that is 455 days after the date of enactment of the Consumer Credit Reporting Reform Act of 1996.

(d) Information required to be disclosed. Any consumer reporting agency that furnishes a consumer report that contains information regarding any case involving the consumer that arises under title 11, United States Code, shall include in the report an identification of the chapter of such title 11 under which such case arises if provided by the source of the information. If any case arising or filed under title 11, United States Code, is withdrawn by the consumer before a final judgment, the consumer reporting agency shall include in the report that such case or filing was withdrawn upon receipt of documentation certifying such withdrawal.

(e) Indication of closure of account by consumer. If a consumer reporting agency is notified pursuant to section 623(a)(4) [§ 1681s-2] that a credit account of a consumer was voluntarily closed by the consumer, the agency shall indicate that fact in any consumer report that includes information related to the account.

(f) Indication of dispute by consumer. If a consumer reporting agency is notified pursuant to section 623(a)(3) [§ 1681s-2] that information regarding a consumer who was furnished to the agency is disputed by the consumer, the agency shall indicate that fact in each consumer report that includes the disputed information.

§ 606. Disclosure of investigative consumer reports [15 U.S.C. § 1681d]

(a) Disclosure of fact of preparation. A person may not procure or cause to be prepared an investigative consumer report on any consumer unless

   (1) it is clearly and accurately disclosed to the consumer that an investigative consumer report including information as to his character, general reputation, personal characteristics and mode of living, whichever are applicable, may be made, and such disclosure

      (A) is made in a writing mailed, or otherwise delivered, to the consumer, not later than three days after the date on which the report was first requested, and

      (B) includes a statement informing the consumer of his right to request the additional disclosures provided for under subsection (b) of this section and the written summary of the rights of the consumer prepared pursuant to section 609(c) [§ 1681g]; and

(2)   the person certifies or has certified to the consumer reporting agency that

      (A)   the person has made the disclosures to the consumer required by paragraph (1); and

      (B)   the person will comply with subsection (b).

(b) Disclosure on request of nature and scope of investigation. Any person who procures or causes to be prepared an investigative consumer report on any consumer shall, upon written request made by the consumer within a reasonable period of time after the receipt by him of the disclosure required by subsection (a)(1) of this section, make a complete and accurate disclosure of the nature and scope of the investigation requested. This disclosure shall be made in a writing mailed, or otherwise delivered, to the consumer not later than five days after the date on which the request for such disclosure was received from the consumer or such report was first requested, whichever is the later.

(c) Limitation on liability upon showing of reasonable procedures for compliance with provisions. No person may be held liable for any violation of subsection (a) or (b) of this section if he shows by a preponderance of the evidence that at the time of the violation he maintained reasonable procedures to assure compliance with subsection (a) or (b) of this section.

(d) Prohibitions.

(1)   Certification. A consumer reporting agency shall not prepare or furnish investigative consumer report unless the agency has received a certification under subsection (a)(2) from the person who requested the report.

(2)   Inquiries. A consumer reporting agency shall not make an inquiry for the purpose of preparing an investigative consumer report on a consumer for employment purposes if the making of the inquiry by an employer

or prospective employer of the consumer would violate any applicable Federal or State equal employment opportunity law or regulation.

(3) Certain public record information. Except as otherwise provided in section 613 [§ 1681k], a consumer reporting agency shall not furnish an investigative consumer report that includes information that is a matter of public record and that relates to an arrest, indictment, conviction, civil judicial action, tax lien, or outstanding judgment, unless the agency has verified the accuracy of the information during the 30-day period ending on the date on which the report is furnished.

(4) Certain adverse information. A consumer reporting agency shall not prepare or furnish an investigative consumer report on a consumer that contains information that is adverse to the interest of the consumer and that is obtained through a personal interview with a neighbor, friend, or associate of the consumer or with another person with whom the consumer is acquainted or who has knowledge of such item of information, unless

(A) the agency has followed reasonable procedures to obtain confirmation of the information, from an additional source that has independent and direct knowledge of the information; or

(B) the person interviewed is the best possible source of the information.

§ 607. Compliance procedures [15 U.S.C. § 1681e]

(a) Identity and purposes of credit users. Every consumer reporting agency shall maintain reasonable procedures designed to avoid violations of section 605 [§ 1681c] and to limit the furnishing of consumer reports to the purposes listed under section 604 [§ 1681b] of this title. These procedures shall require that prospective users of the information identify themselves, certify the purposes for which the information is sought, and certify that the information will be used for no other purpose. Every consumer reporting agency shall make a reasonable effort to verify the identity of a new prospective user and the uses certified by such prospective user prior to furnishing such user a consumer report. No consumer reporting agency may furnish a consumer report to any person if it has reasonable grounds for believing that the consumer report will not be used for a purpose listed in section 604 [§ 1681b] of this title.

(b) Accuracy of report. Whenever a consumer reporting agency prepares a consumer report it shall follow reasonable procedures to assure maximum possible accuracy of the information concerning the individual about whom the report relates.

(c) Disclosure of consumer reports by users allowed. A consumer reporting agency may not prohibit a user of a consumer report furnished by the agency on a consumer from disclosing the contents of the report to the consumer, if adverse action against the consumer has been taken by the user based in whole or in part on the report.

(d) Notice to users and furnishers of information.

    (1)   Notice requirement. A consumer reporting agency shall provide to any person

        (A)   who regularly and in the ordinary course of business furnishes information to the agency with respect to any consumer; or

        (B)   to whom a consumer report is provided by the agency; a notice of such person's responsibilities under this title.

(2)   Content of notice. The Federal Trade Commission shall prescribe the content of notices under paragraph (1), and a consumer reporting agency shall be in compliance with this subsection if it provides a notice under paragraph (1) that is substantially similar to the Federal Trade Commission prescription under this paragraph.

(e) Procurement of consumer report for resale.

(1)   Disclosure. A person may not procure a consumer report for purposes of reselling the report (or any information in the report) unless the person discloses to the consumer reporting agency that originally furnishes the report

(A)   the identity of the end-user of the report (or information); and

(B)   each permissible purpose under section 604 [§ 1681b] for which the report is furnished to the end-user of the report (or information).

(2)   Responsibilities of procurers for resale. A person who procures a consumer report for purposes of reselling the report (or any information in the report) shall

(A)   establish and comply with reasonable procedures designed to ensure that the report (or information) is resold by the person only for a purpose for which the report may be furnished under section 604 [§ 1681b], including by requiring that each person to which the report (or information) is resold and that resells or provides the report (or information) to any other person

(i)   identifies each end user of the resold report (or information);

(ii)   certifies each purpose for which the report (or information) will be used; and

     (iii) certifies that the report (or information) will be used for no other purpose; and

   (B) before reselling the report, make reasonable efforts to verify the identifications and certifications made under subparagraph (A).

  (3) Resale of consumer report to a federal agency or department. Notwithstanding paragraph (1) or (2), a person who procures a consumer report for purposes of reselling the report (or any information in the report) shall not disclose the identity of the end-user of the report under paragraph (1) or (2) if —

   (A) the end user is an agency or department of the United States Government which procures the report from the person for purposes of determining the eligibility of the consumer concerned to receive access or continued access to classified information (as defined in section 604(b)(4)(E)(i)); and

   (B) the agency or department certifies in writing to the person reselling the report that nondisclosure is necessary to protect classified information or the safety of persons employed by or contracting with, or undergoing investigation for work or contracting with the agency or department.

§ 608. Disclosures to governmental agencies [15 U.S.C. § 1681f]

Notwithstanding the provisions of section 604 [§ 1681b] of this title, a consumer reporting agency may furnish identifying information respecting any consumer, limited to his name, address, former addresses, places of employment, or former places of employment, to a governmental agency.

§ 609. Disclosures to consumers [15 U.S.C. § 1681g]

(a) Information on file; sources; report recipients. Every consumer reporting agency shall, upon request, and subject to 610(a)(1) [§ 1681h], clearly and accurately disclose to the consumer:

   (1)   All information in the consumer's file at the time of the request, except that nothing in this paragraph shall be construed to require a consumer reporting agency to disclose to a consumer any information concerning credit scores or any other risk scores or predictors relating to the consumer.

   (2)   The sources of the information; except that the sources of information acquired solely for use in preparing an investigative consumer report and actually used for no other purpose need not be disclosed: Provided, That in the event an action is brought under this title, such sources shall be available to the plaintiff under appropriate discovery procedures in the court in which the action is brought.

   (3)   (A)   Identification of each person (including each end-user identified under section 607(e)(1) [§ 1681e]) that procured a consumer report

             (i)   for employment purposes, during the 2-year period preceding the date on which the request is made; or

             (ii)   for any other purpose, during the 1-year period preceding the date on which the request is made.

          (B)   An identification of a person under subparagraph (A) shall include

             (i)   the name of the person or, if applicable, the trade name (written in full) under which such person conducts business; and

          (ii)   upon request of the consumer, the address and telephone number of the person.

    (C)   Subparagraph (A) does not apply if—

          (i)   the end user is an agency or department of the United States Government that procures the report from the person for purposes of determining the eligibility of the consumer to whom the report relates to receive access or continued access to classified information (as defined in section 604(b)(4)(E)(i)); and

          (ii)   the head of the agency or department makes a written finding as prescribed under section 604(b)(4)(A).

(4)   The dates, original payees, and amounts of any checks upon which is based any adverse characterization of the consumer, included in the file at the time of the disclosure.

(5)   A record of all inquiries received by the agency during the 1-year period preceding the request that identified the consumer in connection with a credit or insurance transaction that was not initiated by the consumer.

(b) Exempt information. The requirements of subsection (a) of this section respecting the disclosure of sources of information and the recipients of consumer reports do not apply to information received or consumer reports furnished prior to the effective date of this title except to the extent that the matter involved is contained in the files of the consumer reporting agency on that date.

(c) Summary of rights required to be included with disclosure.

    (1)   Summary of rights. A consumer reporting agency shall provide to a consumer, with each written disclosure by the agency to the consumer under this section

       (A)   a written summary of all of the rights that the consumer has under this title; and

       (B)   in the case of a consumer reporting agency that compiles and maintains files on consumers on a nationwide basis, a toll-free telephone number established by the agency, at which personnel are accessible to consumers during normal business hours.

(2)   Specific items required to be included. The summary of rights required under paragraph (1) shall include

       (A)   a brief description of this title and all rights of consumers under this title;

       (B)   an explanation of how the consumer may exercise the rights of the consumer under this title;

       (C)   a list of all Federal agencies responsible for enforcing any provision of this title and the address and any appropriate phone number of each such agency, in a form that will assist the consumer in selecting the appropriate agency;

       (D)   a statement that the consumer may have additional rights under State law and that the consumer may wish to contact a State or local consumer protection agency or a State attorney general to learn of those rights; and

       (E)   a statement that a consumer reporting agency is not required to remove accurate derogatory information from a consumer's file, unless the information is outdated under section 605 [§ 1681c] or cannot be verified.

(3)   Form of summary of rights. For purposes of this subsection and any disclosure by a consumer reporting agency

required under this title with respect to consumers' rights, the Federal Trade Commission (after consultation with each Federal agency referred to in section 621(b) [§ 1681s]) shall prescribe the form and content of any such disclosure of the rights of consumers required under this title. A consumer reporting agency shall be in compliance with this subsection if it provides disclosures under paragraph (1) that are substantially similar to the Federal Trade Commission prescription under this paragraph.

(4)   Effectiveness. No disclosures shall be required under this ubsection until the date on which the Federal Trade Commission prescribes the form and content of such disclosures under paragraph (3).

§ 610. Conditions and form of disclosure to consumers [15 U.S.C. § 1681h]

(a) In general.

(1)   Proper identification. A consumer reporting agency shall require, as a condition of making the disclosures required under section 609 [§ 1681g], that the consumer furnish proper identification.

(2)   Disclosure in writing. Except as provided in subsection (b), the disclosures required to be made under section 609 [§ 1681g] shall be provided under that section in writing.

(b) Other forms of disclosure.

(1)   In general. If authorized by a consumer, a consumer reporting agency may make the disclosures required under 609 [§ 1681g]

(A)   other than in writing; and

(B)   in such form as may be

(i)   specified by the consumer in accordance with paragraph (2); and

(ii)   available from the agency.

    (2)   Form. A consumer may specify pursuant to paragraph (1) that disclosures under section 609 [§ 1681g] shall be made

        (A)   in person, upon the appearance of the consumer at the place of business of the consumer reporting agency where disclosures are regularly provided, during normal business hours, and on reasonable notice;

        (B)   by telephone, if the consumer has made a written request for disclosure by telephone;

        (C)   by electronic means, if available from the agency; or

        (D)   by any other reasonable means that is available from the agency.

(c) Trained personnel. Any consumer reporting agency shall provide trained personnel to explain to the consumer any information furnished to him pursuant to section 609 [§ 1681g] of this title.

(d) Persons accompanying consumer. The consumer shall be permitted to be accompanied by one other person of his choosing, who shall furnish reasonable identification. A consumer reporting agency may require the consumer to furnish a written statement granting permission to the consumer reporting agency to discuss the consumer's file in such person's presence.

(e) Limitation of liability. Except as provided in sections 616 and 617 [§§ 1681n and 1681o] of this title, no consumer may bring any action or proceeding in the nature of defamation, invasion of privacy, or negligence with respect to the reporting of information against any consumer reporting agency, any user of information, or any person who furnishes information to a consumer reporting agency, based on information disclosed pursuant to section 609, 610, or 615 [§§ 1681g, 1681h, or

1681m] of this title or based on information disclosed by a user of a consumer report to or for a consumer against whom the user has taken adverse action, based in whole or in part on the report, except as to false information furnished with malice or willful intent to injure such consumer.

§ 611. Procedure in case of disputed accuracy [15 U.S.C. § 1681i]

  (a) Reinvestigations of disputed information.

      (1)   Reinvestigation required.

          (A)   In general. If the completeness or accuracy of any item of information contained in a consumer's file at a consumer reporting agency is disputed by the consumer and the consumer notifies the agency directly of such dispute, the agency shall reinvestigate free of charge and record the current status of the disputed information, or delete the item from the file in accordance with paragraph (5), before the end of the 30-day period beginning on the date on which the agency receives the notice of the dispute from the consumer.

          (B)   Extension of period to reinvestigate. Except as provided in subparagraph (C), the 30-day period described in subparagraph (A) may be extended for not more than 15 additional days if the consumer reporting agency receives information from the consumer during that 30-day period that is relevant to the reinvestigation.

          (C)   Limitations on extension of period to reinvestigate. Subparagraph (B) shall not apply to any reinvestigation in which, during the 30-day period described in subparagraph (A), the information that is the subject of the reinvestigation is found to be inaccurate or incomplete or the consumer reporting agency determines that the information cannot be verified.

(2)　Prompt notice of dispute to furnisher of information.

　　(A)　In general. Before the expiration of the 5-business-day period beginning on the date on which a consumer reporting agency receives notice of a dispute from any consumer in accordance with paragraph (1), the agency shall provide notification of the dispute to any person who provided any item of information in dispute, at the address and in the manner established with the person. The notice shall include all relevant information regarding the dispute that the agency has received from the consumer.

　　(B)　Provision of other information from consumer. The consumer reporting agency shall promptly provide to the person who provided the information in dispute all relevant information regarding the dispute that is received by the agency from the consumer after the period referred to in subparagraph (A) and before the end of the period referred to in paragraph (1)(A).

(3)　Determination that dispute is frivolous or irrelevant.

　　(A)　In general. Notwithstanding paragraph (1), a consumer reporting agency may terminate a reinvestigation of information disputed by a consumer under that paragraph if the agency reasonably determines that the dispute by the consumer is frivolous or irrelevant, including by reason of a failure by a consumer to provide sufficient information to investigate the disputed information.

(B)   Notice of determination. Upon making any determination in accordance with subparagraph (A) that a dispute is frivolous or irrelevant, a consumer reporting agency shall notify the consumer of such determination not later than 5 business days after making such determination, by mail or, if authorized by the consumer for that purpose, by any other means available to the agency.

(C)   Contents of notice. A notice under subparagraph (B) shall include

(i)   the reasons for the determination under subparagraph (A); and

(ii)   identification of any information required to investigate the disputed information, which may consist of a standardized form describing the general nature of such information.

(4)   Consideration of consumer information. In conducting any reinvestigation under paragraph (1) with respect to disputed information in the file of any consumer, the consumer reporting agency shall review and consider all relevant information submitted by the consumer in the period described in paragraph (1)(A) with respect to such disputed information.

(5)   Treatment of inaccurate or unverifiable information.

(A)   In general. If, after any reinvestigation under paragraph (1) of any information disputed by a consumer, an item of the information is found to be inaccurate or incomplete or cannot be verified, the consumer reporting agency shall promptly delete that item of information from the consumer's file or modify that item of information, as appropriate, based on the results of the reinvestigation.

(B) Requirements relating to reinsertion of previously deleted material.

(i) Certification of accuracy of information. If any information is deleted from a consumer's file pursuant to subparagraph (A), the information may not be reinserted in the file by the consumer reporting agency unless the person who furnishes the information certifies that the information is complete and accurate.

(ii) Notice to consumer. If any information that has been deleted from a consumer's file pursuant to subparagraph (A) is reinserted in the file, the consumer reporting agency shall notify the consumer of the reinsertion in writing not later than 5 business days after the reinsertion or, if authorized by the consumer for that purpose, by any other means available to the agency.

(iii) Additional information. As part of, or in addition to, the notice under clause (ii), a consumer reporting agency shall provide to a consumer in writing not later than 5 business days after the date of the reinsertion

(I)   a statement that the disputed information has been reinserted;

(II)   the business name and address of any furnisher of information contacted and the telephone number of such furnisher, if reasonably available, or of any furnisher of information that contacted the consumer reporting agency, in connection with the reinsertion of such information; and

(III)   a notice that the consumer has the right to add a statement to the consumer's file disputing the accuracy or completeness of the disputed information.

(C)   Procedures to prevent reappearance. A consumer reporting agency shall maintain reasonable procedures designed to prevent the reappearance in a consumer's file, and in consumer reports on the consumer, of information that is deleted pursuant to this paragraph (other than information that is reinserted in accordance with subparagraph (B)(i)).

(D)   Automated reinvestigation system. Any consumer reporting agency that compiles and maintains files on consumers on a nationwide basis shall implement an automated system through which furnishers of information to that consumer reporting agency may report the results of a reinvestigation that finds incomplete or inaccurate information in a consumer's file to other such consumer reporting agencies.

(6)   Notice of results of reinvestigation.

(A)   In general. A consumer reporting agency shall provide written notice to a consumer of the results of a reinvestigation under this subsection not later than 5 business days after the completion of the reinvestigation, by mail or, if authorized by the consumer for that purpose, by other means available to the agency.

(B)   Contents. As part of, or in addition to, the notice under subparagraph (A), a consumer reporting agency shall provide to a consumer in writing before the expiration of the 5-day period referred to in subparagraph (A)

(i)   a statement that the reinvestigation is completed;

(ii)   a consumer report that is based upon the consumer's file as that file is revised as a result of the reinvestigation;

(iii)   a notice that, if requested by the consumer, a description of the procedure used to determine the accuracy and completeness of the information shall be provided to the consumer by the agency, including the business name and address of any furnisher of information contacted in connection with such information and the telephone number of such furnisher, if reasonably available;

> (iv) a notice that the consumer has the right to add a statement to the consumer's file disputing the accuracy or completeness of the information; and
>
> (v) a notice that the consumer has the right to request under subsection (d) that the consumer reporting agency furnish notifications under that subsection.

(7) Description of reinvestigation procedure. A consumer reporting agency shall provide to a consumer a description referred to in paragraph (6)(B)(iii) by not later than 15 days after receiving a request from the consumer for that description.

(8) Expedited dispute resolution. If a dispute regarding an item of information in a consumer's file at a consumer reporting agency is resolved in accordance with paragraph (5)(A) by the deletion of the disputed information by not later than 3 business days after the date on which the agency receives notice of the dispute from the consumer in accordance with paragraph (1)(A), then the agency shall not be required to comply with paragraphs (2), (6), and (7) with respect to that dispute if the agency

> (A) provides prompt notice of the deletion to the consumer by telephone;
>
> (B) includes in that notice, or in a written notice that accompanies a confirmation and consumer report provided in accordance with subparagraph (C), a statement of the consumer's right to request under subsection (d) that the agency furnish notifications under that subsection; and

(C)   provides written confirmation of the deletion and a copy of a consumer report on the consumer that is based on the consumer's file after the deletion, not later than 5 business days after making the deletion.

(b) Statement of dispute. If the reinvestigation does not resolve the dispute, the consumer may file a brief statement setting forth the nature of the dispute. The consumer reporting agency may limit such statements to not more than one hundred words if it provides the consumer with assistance in writing a clear summary of the dispute.

(c) Notification of consumer dispute in subsequent consumer reports. Whenever a statement of a dispute is filed, unless there is reasonable grounds to believe that it is frivolous or irrelevant, the consumer reporting agency shall, in any subsequent consumer report containing the information in question, clearly note that it is disputed by the consumer and provide either the consumer's statement or a clear and accurate codification or summary thereof.

(d) Notification of deletion of disputed information. Following any deletion of information which is found to be inaccurate or whose accuracy can no longer be verified or any notation as to disputed information, the consumer reporting agency shall, at the request of the consumer, furnish notification that the item has been deleted or the statement, codification or summary pursuant to subsection (b) or (c) of this section to any person specifically designated by the consumer who has within two years prior thereto received a consumer report for employment purposes, or within six months prior thereto received a consumer report for any other purpose, which contained the deleted or disputed information.

§ 612. Charges for certain disclosures [15 U.S.C. § 1681j]

(a) Reasonable charges allowed for certain disclosures.

    (1)   In general. Except as provided in subsections (b), (c), and (d), a consumer reporting agency may impose a reasonable charge on a consumer

        (A)   for making a disclosure to the consumer pursuant to section 609 [§ 1681g], which charge

            (i)   shall not exceed $8; and

            (ii)   shall be indicated to the consumer before making the disclosure; and

        (B)   for furnishing, pursuant to 611(d) [§ 1681i], following a reinvestigation under section 611(a) [§ 1681i], a statement, codification, or summary to a person designated by the consumer under that section after the 30-day period beginning on the date of notification of the consumer under paragraph (6) or (8) of section 611(a) [§ 1681i] with respect to the reinvestigation, which charge

            (i)   shall not exceed the charge that the agency would impose on each designated recipient for a consumer report; and

            (ii)   shall be indicated to the consumer before furnishing such information.

    (2)   Modification of amount. The Federal Trade Commission shall increase the amount referred to in paragraph (1)(A)(I) on January 1 of each year, based proportionally on changes in the Consumer Price Index, with fractional changes rounded to the nearest fifty cents.

(b) Free disclosure after adverse notice to consumer. Each consumer reporting agency that maintains a file on a consumer shall make all disclosures pursuant to section 609 [§ 1681g] without charge to the consumer if, not later than 60 days after receipt by such consumer of a notification pursuant to section 615 [§ 1681m], or of a notification from a debt collection agency affiliated with that consumer reporting agency stating that the consumer's credit rating may be or has been adversely affected, the consumer makes a request under section 609 [§ 1681g].

(c) Free disclosure under certain other circumstances. Upon the request of the consumer, a consumer reporting agency shall make all disclosures pursuant to section 609 [§ 1681g] once during any 12-month period without charge to that consumer if the consumer certifies in writing that the consumer

   (1)   is unemployed and intends to apply for employment in the 60-day period beginning on the date on which the certification is made;

   (2)   is a recipient of public welfare assistance; or

   (3)   has reason to believe that the file on the consumer at the agency contains inaccurate information due to fraud.

(d) Other charges prohibited. A consumer reporting agency shall not impose any charge on a consumer for providing any notification required by this title or making any disclosure required by this title, except as authorized by subsection (a).

§ 613. Public record information for employment purposes [15 U.S.C. § 1681k]

(a) In general. A consumer reporting agency which furnishes a consumer report for employment purposes and which for that purpose compiles and reports items of information on consumers which are matters of public record and are likely to have an adverse effect upon a consumer's ability to obtain employment shall

(1) at the time such public record information is reported to the user of such consumer report, notify the consumer of the fact that public record information is being reported by the consumer reporting agency, together with the name and address of the person to whom such information is being reported; or

(2) maintain strict procedures designed to insure that whenever public record information which is likely to have an adverse effect on a consumer's ability to obtain employment is reported it is complete and up to date. For purposes of this paragraph, items of public record relating to arrests, indictments, convictions, suits, tax liens, and outstanding judgments shall be considered up to date if the current public record status of the item at the time of the report is reported.

(b) Exemption for national security investigations. Subsection (a) does not apply in the case of an agency or department of the United States Government that seeks to obtain and use a consumer report for employment purposes, if the head of the agency or department makes a written finding as prescribed under section 604(b)(4)(A).

§ 614. Restrictions on investigative consumer reports [15 U.S.C. § 1681l]

Whenever a consumer reporting agency prepares an investigative consumer report, no adverse information in the consumer report (other than information which is a matter of public record) may be included in a subsequent consumer report unless such adverse information has been verified in the process of making such subsequent consumer report, or the adverse information was received within the three-month period preceding the date the subsequent report is furnished.

§ 615. Requirements on users of consumer reports [15 U.S.C. § 1681m]

(a) Duties of users taking adverse actions on the basis of information contained in consumer reports. If any person takes any adverse action with respect to any consumer that is based in whole or in part on any information contained in a consumer report, the person shall

    (1)   provide oral, written, or electronic notice of the adverse action to the consumer;

    (2)   provide to the consumer orally, in writing, or electronically

        (A)   the name, address, and telephone number of the consumer reporting agency (including a toll-free telephone number established by the agency if the agency compiles and maintains files on consumers on a nationwide basis) that furnished the report to the person; and

        (B)   a statement that the consumer reporting agency did not make the decision to take the adverse action and is unable to provide the consumer the specific reasons why the adverse action was taken; and

    (3)   provide to the consumer an oral, written, or electronic notice of the consumer's right

        (A)   to obtain, under section 612 [§ 1681j], a free copy of a consumer report on the consumer from the consumer reporting agency referred to in paragraph (2), which notice shall include an indication of the 60-day period under that section for obtaining such a copy; and

(B) to dispute, under section 611 [§ 1681i], with a consumer reporting agency the accuracy or completeness of any information in a consumer report furnished by the agency.

(b) Adverse action based on information obtained from third parties other than consumer reporting agencies.

(1) In general. Whenever credit for personal, family, or household purposes involving a consumer is denied or the charge for such credit is increased either wholly or partly because of information obtained from a person other than a consumer reporting agency bearing upon the consumer's credit worthiness, credit standing, credit capacity, character, general reputation, personal characteristics, or mode of living, the user of such information shall, within a reasonable period of time, upon the consumer's written request for the reasons for such adverse action received within sixty days after learning of such adverse action, disclose the nature of the information to the consumer. The user of such information shall clearly and accurately disclose to the consumer his right to make such written request at the time such adverse action is communicated to the consumer.

(2) Duties of person taking certain actions based on information provided by affiliate.

(A) Duties, generally. If a person takes an action described in subparagraph (B) with respect to a consumer, based in whole or in part on information described in subparagraph (C), the person shall

(i) notify the consumer of the action, including a statement that the consumer may obtain the information in accordance with clause (ii); and

(ii)   upon a written request from the consumer received within 60 days after transmittal of the notice required by clause (I), disclose to the consumer the nature of the information upon which the action is based by not later than 30 days after receipt of the request.

(B)   Action described. An action referred to in subparagraph (A) is an adverse action described in section 603(k)(1)(A) [§ 1681a], taken in connection with a transaction initiated by the consumer, or any adverse action described in clause (i) or (ii) of section 603(k)(1)(B) [§ 1681a].

(C)   Information described. Information referred to in subparagraph (A)

(i)   except as provided in clause (ii), is information that

(I)   is furnished to the person taking the action by a person related by common ownership or affiliated by common corporate control to the person taking the action; and

(II)   bears on the credit worthiness, credit standing, credit capacity, character, general reputation, personal characteristics, or mode of living of the consumer; and

> (ii)   does not include
>
> > (I)   information solely as to transactions or experiences between the consumer and the person furnishing the information; or
> >
> > (II)   information in a consumer report.

(c) Reasonable procedures to assure compliance. No person shall be held liable for any violation of this section if he shows by a preponderance of the evidence that at the time of the alleged violation he maintained reasonable procedures to assure compliance with the provisions of this section.

(d) Duties of users making written credit or insurance solicitations on the basis of information contained in consumer files.

> (1)   In general. Any person who uses a consumer report on any consumer in connection with any credit or insurance transaction that is not initiated by the consumer, that is provided to that person under section 604(c)(1)(B) [§ 1681b], shall provide with each written solicitation made to the consumer regarding the transaction a clear and conspicuous statement that
>
> > (A)   information contained in the consumer's consumer report was used in connection with the transaction;
> >
> > (B)   the consumer received the offer of credit or insurance because the consumer satisfied the criteria for credit worthiness or insurability under which the consumer was selected for the offer;
> >
> > (C)   if applicable, the credit or insurance may not be extended if, after the consumer responds to the offer, the consumer does not meet the criteria used to select the consumer for the offer or any

applicable criteria bearing on credit worthiness or insurability or does not furnish any required collateral;

(D)   the consumer has a right to prohibit information contained in the consumer's file with any consumer reporting agency from being used in connection with any credit or insurance transaction that is not initiated by the consumer; and

(E)   the consumer may exercise the right referred to in subparagraph

(D)   by notifying a notification system established under section 604(e) [§ 1681b].

(2)   Disclosure of address and telephone number. A statement under paragraph (1) shall include the address and toll-free telephone number of the appropriate notification system established under section 604(e) [§ 1681b].

(3)   Maintaining criteria on file. A person who makes an offer of credit or insurance to a consumer under a credit or insurance transaction described in paragraph (1) shall maintain on file the criteria used to select the consumer to receive the offer, all criteria bearing on credit worthiness or insurability, as applicable, that are the basis for determining whether or not to extend credit or insurance pursuant to the offer, and any requirement for the furnishing of collateral as a condition of the extension of credit or insurance, until the expiration of the 3-year period beginning on the date on which the offer is made to the consumer.

(4)   Authority of federal agencies regarding unfair or deceptive acts or practices not affected. This section is not intended to affect the authority of any Federal or State

agency to enforce a prohibition against unfair or deceptive acts or practices, including the making of false or misleading statements in connection with a credit or insurance transaction that is not initiated by the consumer.

§ 616. Civil liability for willful noncompliance [15 U.S.C. § 1681n]

(a) In general. Any person who willfully fails to comply with any requirement imposed under this title with respect to any consumer is liable to that consumer in an amount equal to the sum of

  (1)   (A)   any actual damages sustained by the consumer as a result of the failure or damages of not less than $100 and not more than $1,000; or

        (B)   in the case of liability of a natural person for obtaining a consumer report under false pretenses or knowingly without a permissible purpose, actual damages sustained by the consumer as a result of the failure or $1,000, whichever is greater;

  (2)   such amount of punitive damages as the court may allow; and

  (3)   in the case of any successful action to enforce any liability under this section, the costs of the action together with reasonable attorney's fees as determined by the court.

(b) Civil liability for knowing noncompliance. Any person who obtains a consumer report from a consumer reporting agency under false pretenses or knowingly without a permissible purpose shall be liable to the consumer reporting agency for actual damages sustained by the consumer reporting agency or $1,000, whichever is greater.

(c) Attorney's fees. Upon a finding by the court that an unsuccessful pleading, motion, or other paper filed in connection with an action under this section was filed in bad faith or for purposes of harassment, the court shall award to the prevailing party attorney's fees reasonable in relation to the work expended in responding to the pleading, motion, or other paper.

§ 617. Civil liability for negligent noncompliance [15 U.S.C. § 1681o]

(a) In general. Any person who is negligent in failing to comply with any requirement imposed under this title with respect to any consumer is liable to that consumer in an amount equal to the sum of

    (1)   any actual damages sustained by the consumer as a result of the failure;

    (2)   in the case of any successful action to enforce any liability under this section, the costs of the action together with reasonable attorney's fees as determined by the court.

(b) Attorney's fees. On a finding by the court that an unsuccessful leading, motion, or other paper filed in connection with an action under this section was filed in bad faith or for purposes of harassment, the court shall award to the prevailing party attorney's fees reasonable in relation to the work expended in responding to the pleading, motion, or other paper.

§ 618. Jurisdiction of courts; limitation of actions [15 U.S.C. § 1681p]

An action to enforce any liability created under this title may be brought in any appropriate United States district court without regard to the amount in controversy, or in any other court of competent jurisdiction, within two years from the date on which the liability arises, except that where a defendant has materially and willfully misrepresented any information required under this title to be disclosed to an individual and the information so misrepresented is material to the establishment of the defendant's liability to that individual under this title, the action may be brought at any time within two years after discovery by the individual of the misrepresentation.

§ 619. Obtaining information under false pretenses [15 U.S.C. § 1681q]

Any person who knowingly and willfully obtains information on a consumer from a consumer reporting agency under false pretenses shall be fined under title 18, United States Code, imprisoned for not more than 2 years, or both.

§ 620. Unauthorized disclosures by officers or employees [15 U.S.C. § 1681r]

Any officer or employee of a consumer reporting agency who knowingly and willfully provides information concerning an individual from the agency's files to a person not authorized to receive that information shall be fined under title 18, United States Code, imprisoned for not more than 2 years, or both.

§ 621. Administrative enforcement [15 U.S.C. § 1681s]

(a) (1) Enforcement by Federal Trade Commission. Compliance with the requirements imposed under this title shall be enforced under the Federal Trade Commission Act [15 U.S.C. §§ 41 et seq.] by the Federal Trade Commission with respect to consumer reporting agencies and all other persons subject thereto, except to the extent that enforcement of the requirements imposed under this title is specifically committed to some other government agency under subsection (b) hereof. For the purpose of the exercise by the Federal Trade Commission of its functions and powers under the Federal Trade Commission Act, a violation of any requirement or prohibition imposed under this title shall constitute an unfair or deceptive act or practice in commerce in violation of section 5(a) of the Federal Trade Commission Act [15 U.S.C. § 45(a)] and shall be subject to enforcement by the Federal Trade

Commission under section 5(b) thereof [15 U.S.C. § 45(b)] with respect to any consumer reporting agency or person subject to enforcement by the Federal Trade Commission pursuant to this subsection, irrespective of whether that person is engaged in commerce or meets any other jurisdictional tests in the Federal Trade Commission Act. The Federal Trade Commission shall have such procedural, investigative, and enforcement powers, including the power to issue procedural rules in enforcing compliance with the requirements imposed under this title and to require the filing of reports, the production of documents, and the appearance of witnesses as though the applicable terms and conditions of the Federal Trade Commission Act were part of this title. Any person violating any of the provisions of this title shall be subject to the penalties and entitled to the privileges and immunities provided in the Federal Trade Commission Act as though the applicable terms and provisions thereof were part of this title.

(2)   (A)   In the event of a knowing violation, which constitutes a pattern or practice of violations of this title, the Commission may commence a civil action to recover a civil penalty in a district court of the United States against any person that violates this title. In such action, such person shall be liable for a civil penalty of not more than $2,500 per violation.

        (B)   In determining the amount of a civil penalty under subparagraph (A), the court shall take into account the degree of culpability, any history of prior such conduct, ability to pay, effect on ability to continue to do business, and such other matters as justice may require.

(3)   Notwithstanding paragraph (2), a court may not impose any civil penalty on a person for a violation of section 623(a)(1) [§ 1681s-2] unless the person has been enjoined from committing the violation, or ordered not to commit the violation, in an action or proceeding brought by or on behalf of the Federal Trade Commission, and has violated the injunction or order, and the court may not impose any civil penalty for any violation occurring before the date of the violation of the injunction or order.

(4)   Neither the Commission nor any other agency referred to in subsection (b) may prescribe trade regulation rules or other regulations with respect to this title.

(b) Enforcement by other agencies. Compliance with the requirements imposed under this title with respect to consumer reporting agencies, persons who use consumer reports from such agencies, persons who furnish information to such agencies, and users of information that are subject to subsection (d) of section 615 [§ 1681m] shall be enforced under

(1)   section 8 of the Federal Deposit Insurance Act [12 U.S.C. § 1818], in the case of

(A)   national banks, and Federal branches and Federal agencies of foreign banks, by the Office of the Comptroller of the Currency;

(B)   member banks of the Federal Reserve System (other than national banks), branches and agencies of foreign banks (other than Federal branches, Federal agencies, and insured State branches of foreign banks), commercial lending companies owned or controlled by foreign banks, and organizations operating under section 25 or 25(a) [25A] of the Federal Reserve Act [12 U.S.C. §§ 601 et seq., §§ 611 et seq], by the Board of Governors of the Federal Reserve System; and

(C)   banks insured by the Federal Deposit Insurance Corporation (other than members of the Federal Reserve System) and insured State branches of foreign banks, by the Board of Directors of the Federal Deposit Insurance Corporation;

(2)   section 8 of the Federal Deposit Insurance Act [12 U.S.C. § 1818], by the Director of the Office of Thrift Supervision, in the case of a savings association the deposits of which are insured by the Federal Deposit Insurance Corporation;

(3)   the Federal Credit Union Act [12 U.S.C. §§ 1751 et seq.], by the Administrator of the National Credit Union Administration [National Credit Union Administration Board] with respect to any Federal credit union;

(4)   subtitle IV of title 49 [49 U.S.C. §§ 10101 et seq.], by the Secretary of Transportation, with respect to all carriers subject to the jurisdiction of the Surface Transportation Board;

(5)   the Federal Aviation Act of 1958 [49 U.S.C. Appx §§ 1301 et seq.], by the Secretary of Transportation with respect to any air carrier or foreign air carrier subject to that Act [49 U.S.C. Appx §§ 1301 et seq.]; and

(6)   the Packers and Stockyards Act, 1921 [7 U.S.C. §§ 181 et seq.] (except as provided in section 406 of that Act [7

U.S.C. §§ 226 and 227]), by the Secretary of Agriculture with respect to any activities subject to that Act.

The terms used in paragraph (1) that are not defined in this title or otherwise defined in section 3(s) of the Federal Deposit Insurance Act (12 U.S.C. § 1813(s)) shall have the meaning given to them in section 1(b) of the International Banking Act of 1978 (12 U.S.C. § 3101).

(c) State action for violations.

(1)   Authority of states. In addition to such other remedies as are provided under State law, if the chief law enforcement officer of a State, or an official or agency designated by a State, has reason to believe that any person has violated or is violating this title, the State

(A)   may bring an action to enjoin such violation in any appropriate United States district court or in any other court of competent jurisdiction;

(B)   subject to paragraph (5), may bring an action on behalf of the residents of the State to recover

(i)   damages for which the person is liable to such residents under sections 616 and 617 [§§ 1681n and 1681o] as a result of the violation;

(ii)   in the case of a violation of section 623(a) [§ 1681s-2], damages for which the person would, but for section 623(c) [§ 1681s-2], be liable to such residents as a result of the violation; or

(iii)   damages of not more than $1,000 for each willful or negligent violation; and

(C)   in the case of any successful action under subparagraph (A) or (B), shall be awarded the costs of the action and reasonable attorney fees as determined by the court.

(2)   Rights of federal regulators. The State shall serve prior written notice of any action under paragraph (1) upon the Federal Trade Commission or the appropriate Federal regulator determined under subsection (b) and provide the Commission or appropriate Federal regulator with a copy of its complaint, except in any case in which such prior notice is not feasible, in which case the State shall serve such notice immediately upon instituting such action. The Federal Trade Commission or appropriate Federal regulator shall have the right

(A)   to intervene in the action;

(B)   upon so intervening, to be heard on all matters arising therein;

(C)   to remove the action to the appropriate United States district court; and

(D)   to file petitions for appeal.

(3)   Investigatory powers. For purposes of bringing any action under this subsection, nothing in this subsection shall prevent the chief law enforcement officer, or an official or agency designated by a State, from exercising the powers conferred on the chief law enforcement officer or such official by the laws of such State to conduct investigations or to administer oaths or affirmations or to compel the attendance of witnesses or the production of documentary and other evidence.

(4)   Limitation on state action while federal action pending. If the Federal Trade Commission or the appropriate Federal regulator has instituted a civil action or an administrative action under section 8 of the Federal

Deposit Insurance Act for a violation of this title, no State may, during the pendency of such action, bring an action under this section against any defendant named in the complaint of the Commission or the appropriate Federal regulator for any violation of this title that is alleged in that complaint.

(5) Limitations on state actions for violation of section 623(a)(1) [§ 1681s-2].

(A) Violation of injunction required. A State may not bring an action against a person under paragraph (1)(B) for a violation of section 623(a)(1) [§ 1681s-2], unless

(i) the person has been enjoined from committing the violation, in an action brought by the State under paragraph (1)(A); and

(ii) the person has violated the injunction.

(B) Limitation on damages recoverable. In an action against a person under paragraph (1)(B) for a violation of section 623(a)(1) [§ 1681s-2], a State may not recover any damages incurred before the date of the violation of an injunction on which the action is based.

(d) Enforcement under other authority. For the purpose of the exercise by any agency referred to in subsection (b) of this section of its powers under any Act referred to in that subsection, a violation of any requirement imposed under this title shall be deemed to be a violation of a requirement imposed under that Act. In addition to its powers under any provision of law specifically referred to in subsection (b) of this section, each of the agencies referred to in that subsection may exercise, for the purpose of enforcing compliance with any requirement imposed under this title any other authority conferred on it by law. Notwithstanding the preceding, no agency referred to in subsection (b) may conduct an examination of a bank, savings association, or credit union regarding compliance with the provisions of this title, except in response to a complaint (or if the agency otherwise has knowledge) that the bank, savings association, or credit union has violated a provision of this title, in which case, the agency may conduct an examination as necessary to investigate the complaint. If an agency determines during an investigation in response to a complaint that a violation of this title has occurred, the agency may, during its next 2 regularly scheduled examinations of the bank, savings association, or credit union, examine for compliance with this title.

(e) Interpretive authority. The Board of Governors of the Federal Reserve System may issue interpretations of any provision of this title as such provision may apply to any persons identified under paragraph (1), (2), and (3) of subsection (b), or to the holding companies and affiliates of such persons, in consultation with Federal agencies identified in paragraphs (1), (2), and (3) of subsection (b).

§ 622. Information on overdue child support obligations [15 U.S.C. § 1681s-1]

Notwithstanding any other provision of this title, a consumer reporting agency shall include in any consumer report furnished by the agency in accordance with section 604 [§ 1681b] of this title, any information on the failure of the consumer to pay overdue support which

(1) is provided

   (A)   to the consumer reporting agency by a State or local child support enforcement agency; or

(B)   to the consumer reporting agency and verified by any local, State, or Federal government agency; and

(2) antedates the report by 7 years or less.

§ 623. Responsibilities of furnishers of information to consumer reporting agencies [15 U.S.C. § 1681s-2]

(a) Duty of furnishers of information to provide accurate information.

    (1)   Prohibition.

        (A)   Reporting information with actual knowledge of errors. A person shall not furnish any information relating to a consumer to any consumer reporting agency if the person knows or consciously avoids knowing that the information is inaccurate.

        (B)   Reporting information after notice and confirmation of errors. A person shall not furnish information relating to a consumer to any consumer reporting agency if

            (i)   the person has been notified by the consumer, at the address specified by the person for such notices, that specific information is inaccurate; and

            (ii)   the information is, in fact, inaccurate.

        (C)   No address requirement. A person who clearly and conspicuously specifies to the consumer an address for notices referred to in subparagraph (B) shall not be subject to subparagraph (A); however, nothing in subparagraph (B) shall require a person to specify such an address.

    (2)   Duty to correct and update information. A person who

        (A)   regularly and in the ordinary course of business furnishes information to one or more consumer reporting agencies about the person's transactions or experiences with any consumer; and

    (B)   has furnished to a consumer reporting agency information that the person determines is not complete or accurate, shall promptly notify the consumer reporting agency of that determination and provide to the agency any corrections to that information, or any additional information, that is necessary to make the information provided by the person to the agency complete and accurate, and shall not thereafter furnish to the agency any of the information that remains not complete or accurate.

(3)   Duty to provide notice of dispute. If the completeness or accuracy of any information furnished by any person to any consumer reporting agency is disputed to such person by a consumer, the person may not furnish the information to any consumer reporting agency without notice that such information is disputed by the consumer.

(4)   Duty to provide notice of closed accounts. A person who regularly and in the ordinary course of business furnishes information to a consumer reporting agency regarding a consumer who has a credit account with that person shall notify the agency of the voluntary closure of the account by the consumer, in information regularly furnished for the period in which the account is closed.

(5)   Duty to provide notice of delinquency of accounts. A person who furnishes information to a consumer reporting agency regarding a delinquent account being placed for collection, charged to profit or loss, or subjected to any similar action shall, not later than 90 days

after furnishing the information, notify the agency of the month and year of the commencement of the delinquency that immediately preceded the action.

(b) Duties of furnishers of information upon notice of dispute.

    (1)   In general. After receiving notice pursuant to section 611(a)(2) [§ 1681i] of a dispute with regard to the completeness or accuracy of any information provided by a person to a consumer reporting agency, the person shall

        (A)   conduct an investigation with respect to the disputed information;

        (B)   review all relevant information provided by the consumer reporting agency pursuant to section 611(a)(2) [§ 1681i];

        (C)   report the results of the investigation to the consumer reporting agency; and

        (D)   if the investigation finds that the information is incomplete or inaccurate, report those results to all other consumer reporting agencies to which the person furnished the information and that compile and maintain files on consumers on a nationwide basis.

    (2)   Deadline. A person shall complete all investigations, reviews, and reports required under paragraph (1) regarding information provided by the person to a consumer reporting agency, before the expiration of the period under section 611(a)(1) [§ 1681i] within which the consumer reporting agency is required to complete actions required by that section regarding that information.

(c) Limitation on liability. Sections 616 and 617 [§§ 1681n and 1681o] do not apply to any failure to comply with subsection (a), except as provided in section 621(c)(1)(B) [§ 1681s].

(d) Limitation on enforcement. Subsection (a) shall be enforced exclusively under section 621 [§ 1681s] by the Federal agencies and officials and the State officials identified in that section.

§ 624. Relation to State laws [15 U.S.C. § 1681t]

(a) In general. Except as provided in subsections (b) and (c), this title does not annul, alter, affect, or exempt any person subject to the provisions of this title from complying with the laws of any State with respect to the collection, distribution, or use of any information on consumers, except to the extent that those laws are inconsistent with any provision of this title, and then only to the extent of the inconsistency.

(b) General exceptions. No requirement or prohibition may be imposed under the laws of any State

    (1) with respect to any subject matter regulated under

        (A) subsection (c) or (e) of section 604 [§ 1681b], relating to the prescreening of consumer reports;

        (B) section 611 [§ 1681i], relating to the time by which a consumer reporting agency must take any action, including the provision of notification to a consumer or other person, in any procedure related to the disputed accuracy of information in a consumer's file, except that this subparagraph shall not apply to any State law in effect on the date of enactment of the Consumer Credit Reporting Reform Act of 1996;

(C)   subsections (a) and (b) of section 615 [§ 1681m], relating to the duties of a person who takes any adverse action with respect to a consumer;

(D)   section 615(d) [§ 1681m], relating to the duties of persons who use a consumer report of a consumer in connection with any credit or insurance transaction that is not initiated by the consumer and that consists of a firm offer of credit or insurance;

(E)   section 605 [§ 1681c], relating to information contained in consumer reports, except that this subparagraph shall not apply to any State law in effect on the date of enactment of the Consumer Credit Reporting Reform Act of 1996; or

(F)   section 623 [§ 1681s-2], relating to the responsibilities of persons who furnish information to consumer reporting agencies, except that this paragraph shall not apply

    (i)   with respect to section 54A(a) of chapter 93 of the Massachusetts Annotated Laws (as in effect on the date of enactment of the Consumer Credit Reporting Reform Act of 1996); or

    (ii)   with respect to section 1785.25(a) of the California Civil Code (as in effect on the date of enactment of the Consumer Credit Reporting Reform Act of 1996);

(2)   with respect to the exchange of information among persons affiliated by common ownership or common corporate control, except that this paragraph shall not apply with respect to subsection (a) or (c)(1) of section 2480e of title 9, Vermont Statutes Annotated (as in effect

on the date of enactment of the Consumer Credit Reporting Reform Act of 1996); or

(3)   with respect to the form and content of any disclosure required to be made under section 609(c) [§ 1681g].

(c) Definition of firm offer of credit or insurance. Notwithstanding any definition of the term "firm offer of credit or insurance" (or any equivalent term) under the laws of any State, the definition of that term contained in section 603(l) [§ 1681a] shall be construed to apply in the enforcement and interpretation of the laws of any State governing consumer reports.

(d) Limitations. Subsections (b) and (c)

(1)   do not affect any settlement, agreement, or consent judgment between any State Attorney General and any consumer reporting agency in effect on the date of enactment of the Consumer Credit Reporting Reform Act of 1996; and

(2)   do not apply to any provision of State law (including any provision of a State constitution) that

(A)   is enacted after January 1, 2004;

(B)   states explicitly that the provision is intended to supplement this title; and

(C)   gives greater protection to consumers than is provided under this title.

§ 625. Disclosures to FBI for counterintelligence purposes [15 U.S.C.§ 1681u]

(a) Identity of financial institutions. Notwithstanding section 604 [§ 1681b] or any other provision of this title, a consumer reporting agency shall furnish to the Federal Bureau of Investigation the names and addresses of all financial institutions (as that term is defined in section 1101 of the Right to

Financial Privacy Act of 1978 [12 U.S.C. § 3401]) at which a consumer maintains or has maintained an account, to the extent that information is in the files of the agency, when presented with a written request for that information, signed by the Director of the Federal Bureau of Investigation, or the Director's designee, which certifies compliance with this section. The Director or the Director's designee may make such a certification only if the Director or the Director's designee has determined in writing that

(1)   such information is necessary for the conduct of an authorized foreign counterintelligence investigation; and

(2)   there are specific and articulable facts giving reason to believe that the consumer

    (A)   is a foreign power (as defined in section 101 of the Foreign Intelligence Surveillance Act of 1978 [50 U.S.C. § 1801]) or a person who is not a United States person (as defined in such section 101) and is an official of a foreign power; or

    (B)   is an agent of a foreign power and is engaging or has engaged in an act of international terrorism (as that term is defined in section 101(c) of the Foreign Intelligence Surveillance Act of 1978 [50 U.S.C. § 1801(c)]) or clandestine intelligence activities that involve or may involve a violation of criminal statutes of the United States.

(b) Identifying information. Notwithstanding the provisions of section 604 [§ 1681b] or any other provision of this title, a consumer reporting agency shall furnish identifying information respecting a consumer, limited to name, address, former addresses, places of employment, or former places of employment, to the Federal Bureau of Investigation when presented with a written request, signed by the Director or the Director's designee, which certifies compliance with this subsection. The Director or the Director's designee may make such a certification only if the Director or the Director's designee has determined in writing that

(1)   such information is necessary to the conduct of an authorized counterintelligence investigation; and

(2)   there is information giving reason to believe that the consumer has been, or is about to be, in contact with a foreign power or an agent of a foreign power (as defined in section 101 of the Foreign Intelligence Surveillance Act of 1978 [50 U.S.C. § 1801]).

(c)   Court order for disclosure of consumer reports. Notwithstanding section 604 [§ 1681b] or any other provision of this title, if requested in writing by the Director of the Federal Bureau of Investigation, or a designee of the Director, a court may issue an order ex parte directing a consumer reporting agency to furnish a consumer report to the Federal Bureau of Investigation, upon a showing in camera that

(1)   the consumer report is necessary for the conduct of an authorized foreign counterintelligence investigation; and

(2)   there are specific and articulable facts giving reason to believe that the consumer whose consumer report is sought

(A)   is an agent of a foreign power, and

(B)   is engaging or has engaged in an act of international terrorism (as that term is defined in section 101(c) of the Foreign Intelligence Surveillance Act of 1978 [50 U.S.C. § 1801(c)]) or clandestine intelligence activities that involve or may involve a violation of criminal statutes of the United States. The terms of an order issued under this subsection shall not disclose that the order is issued for purposes of a counterintelligence investigation.

(d) Confidentiality. No consumer reporting agency or officer, employee, or agent of a consumer reporting agency shall disclose to any person, other than those officers, employees, or agents of a consumer reporting agency necessary to fulfill the requirement to disclose information to the Federal Bureau of Investigation under this section, that the Federal Bureau of Investigation has sought or obtained the identity of financial institutions or a consumer report respecting any consumer under subsection (a), (b), or (c), and no consumer reporting agency or officer, employee, or agent of a consumer reporting agency shall include in any consumer report any information that would indicate that the Federal Bureau of Investigation has sought or obtained such information or a consumer report.

(e) Payment of fees. The Federal Bureau of Investigation shall, subject to the availability of appropriations, pay to the consumer reporting agency assembling or providing report or information in accordance with procedures established under this section a fee for reimbursement for such costs as are reasonably necessary and which have been directly incurred in searching, reproducing, or transporting books, papers, records, or otherdata required or requested to be produced under this section.

(f) Limit on dissemination. The Federal Bureau of Investigation may not disseminate information obtained pursuant to this section outside of the Federal Bureau of Investigation, except to other Federal agencies as may be necessary for the approval or conduct of a foreign counterintelligence investigation, or, where the information concerns a person subject to the Uniform Code of Military Justice, to appropriate investigative authorities within the military department concerned as may be necessary for the conduct of a joint foreign counterintelligence investigation.

(g) Rules of construction. Nothing in this section shall be construed to prohibit information from being furnished by the Federal Bureau of Investigation pursuant to a subpoena or court order, in connection with a judicial or administrative proceeding to enforce the provisions of this Act. Nothing in this section shall be construed to authorize or permit the withholding of information from the Congress.

(h) Reports to Congress. On a semiannual basis, the Attorney General shall fully inform the Permanent Select Committee on Intelligence and the Committee on Banking, Finance and Urban Affairs of the House of Representatives, and the Select Committee on Intelligence and the Committee on Banking, Housing, and Urban Affairs of the Senate concerning all requests made pursuant to subsections (a), (b), and (c).

(i) Damages. Any agency or department of the United States obtaining or disclosing any consumer reports, records, or information contained therein in violation of this section is liable to the consumer to whom such consumer reports, records, or information relate in an amount equal to the sum of

(1) $100, without regard to the volume of consumer reports, records, or information involved;

(2) any actual damages sustained by the consumer as a result of the disclosure;

(3) if the violation is found to have been willful or intentional, such punitive damages as a court may allow; and

(4) in the case of any successful action to enforce liability under this subsection, the costs of the action, together with reasonable attorney fees, as determined by the court.

(j) Disciplinary actions for violations. If a court determines that any agency or department of the United States has violated any provision of this section and the court finds that the circumstances surrounding the violation raise questions of whether or not an officer or employee of the agency or department acted willfully or intentionally with respect to the violation, the agency or department shall promptly initiate a proceeding to determine whether or not disciplinary action is warranted against the officer or employee who was responsible for the violation.

(k) Good-faith exception. Notwithstanding any other provision of this title, any consumer reporting agency or agent or employee thereof making disclosure of consumer reports or identifying information pursuant to this subsection in good-faith reliance upon a certification of the Federal Bureau of Investigation pursuant to provisions of this section shall not be liable to any person for such disclosure under this title, the constitution of any State, or any law or regulation of any State or any political subdivision of any State.

(l) Limitation of remedies. Notwithstanding any other provision of this title, the remedies and sanctions set forth in this section shall be the only judicial remedies and sanctions for violation of this section.

(m) Injunctive relief. In addition to any other remedy contained in this section, injunctive relief shall be available to require compliance with the procedures of this section. In the event of any successful action under this subsection, costs together with reasonable attorney fees, as determined by the court, may be recovered.

*   *   *

Legislative History
House Reports: No. 91-975 (Comm. on Banking and Currency) and No. 91-1587 (Comm. of Conference)

Senate Reports: No. 91-1139 accompanying S. 3678 (Comm. on Banking and Currency)

Congressional Record, Vol. 116 (1970)

> May 25, considered and passed House.
> Sept. 18, considered and passed Senate, amended.
> Oct. 9, Senate agreed to conference report.
> Oct. 13, House agreed to conference report.

Enactment:
Public Law No. 91-508 (October 26, 1970):

Amendments: Public Law Nos.
95-473 (October 17, 1978)
95-598 (November 6, 1978)
98-443 (October 4, 1984)
101-73 (August 9, 1989)
102-242 (December 19, 1991)
102-537 (October 27, 1992)
102-550 (October 28, 1992)
103-325 (September 23, 1994)
104-88 (December 29, 1995)
104-93 (January 6, 1996)
104-193 (August 22, 1996)
104-208 (September 30, 1996)
105-107 (November 20, 1997)
105-347 (November 2, 1998)

           *   *   *

1. The reporting periods have been lengthened for certain adverse information pertaining to U.S. Government insured or guaranteed student loans, or pertaining to national direct student loans. See sections 430A(f) and 463(c)(3) of the Higher Education Act of 1965, 20 U.S.C. 1080a(f) and 20 U.S.C. 1087cc(c)(3), respectively.

**Should read "paragraphs (4) and (5) ..." Prior Section 605(a)(6) was amended and redesignated as Section 605(a)(5) in November 1998.

Appendix K—Federal Driver's Privacy Protection Act
(18 U.S.C. Section 2721 et. Seq.)

Sec. 2721. Prohibition on release and use of certain personal information from State motor vehicle records.

(a) In General.—Except as provided in subsection (b), a State department of motor vehicles, and any officer, employee, or contractor, thereof, shall not knowingly disclose or otherwise make available to any person or entity personal information about any individual obtained by the department in connection with a motor vehicle record.

(b) Permissible Uses.—Personal information referred to in subsection (a) shall be disclosed for use in connection with matters of motor vehicle or driver safety and theft, motor vehicle emissions, motor vehicle product alterations, recalls, or advisories, performance monitoring of motor vehicles and dealers by motor vehicle manufacturers, and removal of non-owner records from the original owner records of motor vehicle manufacturers to carry out the purposes of title I and IV of the Anti-Car Theft Act of 1992, the Automobile Information Disclosure Act (15 U.S.C. 1231 et seq.), the Clean Air Act (42 U.S.C. 7401 et seq.), and chapters 301, 305, and 321-331 of title 49 (49 U.S.C.S. 30101 et seq., 30501 et seq., 32101 et seq.-33101 et seq.), and may be disclosed as follows:

(1)   For use by any government agency, including any court or law enforcement agency, in carrying out its functions, or any private person or entity acting on behalf of a Federal, State, or local agency in carrying out its functions.

(2)   For use in connection with matters of motor vehicle or driver safety and theft; motor vehicle emissions; motor vehicle product alterations, recalls, or advisories; performance monitoring of motor vehicles, motor vehicle parts and dealers; motor vehicle market research activities, including survey research; and removal of non-owner records from the original owner records of motor vehicle manufacturers.

(3)   For use in the normal course of business by a legitimate business or its agents, employees, or contractors, but only—

    A.   to verify the accuracy of personal information submitted by the individual to the business or its agents, employees, or contractors; and

    B.   if such information as so submitted is not correct or is no longer correct, to obtain the correct information, but only for the purposes of preventing fraud by, pursuing legal remedies against, or recovering on a debt or security interest against, the individual.

(4)   For use in connection with any civil, criminal, administrative, or arbitral proceeding in any Federal, State, or local court or agency or before any self-regulatory body, including the service of process, investigation in anticipation of litigation, and the execution or enforcement of judgments and orders, or pursuant to an order of a Federal, State, or local court.

(5)   For use in research activities, and for use in producing statistical reports, so long as the personal information is not published, redisclosed, or used to contact individuals.

(6)   For use by any insurer or insurance support organization, or by a self-insured entity, or its agents, employees, or contractors, in connection with claims investigation activities, antifraud activities, rating or underwriting.

(7)   For use in providing notice to the owners of towed or impounded vehicles.

(8)   For use by any licensed private investigative agency or licensed security service for any purpose permitted under this subsection.

(9)   For use by an employer or its agent or insurer to obtain or verify information relating to a holder of a commercial driver's license that is required under Chapter 313 of Title 49.

(10)   For use in connection with the operation of private toll transportation facilities.

(11)   For any other use in response to requests for individual motor vehicle records if the motor vehicle department has provided in a clear and conspicuous manner on forms for issuance or renewal of operator's permits, titles, registrations, or identification cards, notice that personal information collected by the department may be disclosed to any business or person, and has provided in a clear and conspicuous manner on such forms an opportunity to prohibit such disclosures.

(12)   For bulk distribution for surveys, marketing or solicitations if the motor vehicle department has implemented methods and procedures to ensure that—

A.   individuals are provided an opportunity, in a clear and conspicuous manner, to prohibit such uses; and

B.   the information will be used, rented, or sold solely for bulk distribution for surveys, marketing, and solicitations, and that surveys, marketing, and solicitations will not be directed at those individuals who have requested in a timely fashion that they not be directed at them.

(13)   For use by any requester, if the requester demonstrates it has obtained the written consent of the individual to whom the information pertains.

(14)   For any other use specifically authorized under the law of the State that holds the record, if such use is related to the operation of a motor vehicle or public safety.

(c) Resale or Redisclosure.—An authorized recipient of personal information (except a recipient under subsection (b)(11) or (12)) may resell or redisclose the information only for a use permitted under subsection (b) (but not for uses under subsection (b)(11) or (12)). An authorized recipient under subsection (b)(11) may resell or redisclose personal information for any purpose. An authorized recipient under subsection (b)(12) may resell or redisclose personal information pursuant to subsection (b)(12). Any authorized recipient (except a recipient under subsection (b)(11)) that resells or rediscloses personal information covered by this title must keep for a period of 5 years records identifying each person or entity that receives information and the permitted purpose for which the information will be used and must make such records available to the motor vehicle department upon request.

(d) Waiver Procedures.—A State motor vehicle department may establish and carry out procedures under which the department or its agents, upon receiving a request for personal information that does not fall within one of the exceptions in subsection (b), may mail a copy of the request to the individual about whom the information was requested, informing such individual of the request, together with a statement to the effect that the information will not be released unless the individual waives such individual's right to privacy under this section.

Sec. 2722. Additional unlawful acts

(a) Procurement for Unlawful Purpose.—It shall be unlawful for any person knowingly to obtain or disclose personal information, from a motor vehicle record, for any use not permitted under section 2721(b) of this title.

(b) False Representation.—It shall be unlawful for any person to make false representation to obtain any personal information from an individual's motor vehicle record.

Sec. 2723. Penalties

(a) Criminal Fine.—A person who knowingly violates this chapter shall be fined under this title.

(b) Violations by State Department of Motor Vehicles.—Any State department of motor vehicles that has a policy or practice of substantial noncompliance with this chapter shall be subject to a civil penalty imposed by the Attorney General of not more than $5,000 a day for each day of substantial noncompliance.

Sec. 2724. Civil action

(a) Cause of Action.—A person who knowingly obtains, discloses or uses personal information, from a motor vehicle record, for a purpose not permitted under this chapter shall be liable to the individual to whom the information pertains, who may bring a civil action in a United States district court.

(b) Remedies.—The court may award—

   (1)   actual damages, but not less than liquidated damages in the amount of $2,500;

   (2)   punitive damages upon proof of willful or reckless disregard of the law;

   (3)   reasonable attorneys' fees and other litigation costs reasonably incurred; and

   (4)   such other preliminary and equitable relief as the court determines to be appropriate.

Sec. 2725. Definitions

In this chapter—

(1) "motor vehicle record" means any record that pertains to a motor vehicle operator's permit, motor vehicle title, motor vehicle registration, or identification card issued by a department of motor vehicles;

(2) "person" means an individual, organization or entity, but does not include a State or agency thereof; and

(3) "personal information" means information that identifies an individual, including an individual's photograph, social security number, driver identification number, name, address (but not the 5-digit zip code), telephone number, and medical or disability information, but does not include information on vehicular accidents, driving violations, and driver's status.

The amendments made by section 300002 shall become effective on the date that is 3 years after the date of enactment of this Act (Sept. 13, 1994). After the effective date, if a State has implemented a procedure under section 2721(b)(11) and (12) of title 18, United States Code, as added by section 300002(a), for prohibiting disclosures or uses of personal information, and the procedure otherwise meets the requirements of subsection (b)(11) and (12), the State shall be in compliance with subsection (b)(11) and (12) even if the procedure is not available to individuals until they renew their license, title, registration or identification card, so long as the State provides some other procedure for individuals to contact the State on their own initiative to prohibit such uses or disclosures. Prior to the effective date, personal information covered by the amendment made by section 300002 may be released consistent with State law or practice.

Pub. L. 103-322, title XXX, Sec. 300002(a), Sept. 13, 1994, 108 Stat. 2102.

Appendix L—Fair Debt Collection Practices Act

As amended by Public Law 104-208, 110 Stat. 3009 (Sept. 30, 1996)

To amend the Consumer Credit Protection Act to prohibit abusive practices by debt collectors.

Be it enacted by the Senate and House of Representatives of the United States of America in Congress assembled, That the Consumer Credit Protection Act (15 U.S.C. 1601 et seq.) is amended by adding at the end thereof the following new title:

TITLE VIII—DEBT COLLECTION PRACTICES [Fair Debt Collection Practices Act]

§ 801. Short Title [15 USC 1601 note]

This title may be cited as the "Fair Debt Collection Practices Act."

§ 802. Congressional findings and declarations of purpose [15 USC 1692]

(a)   There is abundant evidence of the use of abusive, deceptive, and unfair debt collection practices by many debt collectors. Abusive debt collection practices contribute to the number of personal bankruptcies, to marital instability, to the loss of jobs, and to invasions of individual privacy.

(b)   Existing laws and procedures for redressing these injuries are inadequate to protect consumers.

(c)   Means other than misrepresentation or other abusive debt collection practices are available for the effective collection of debts.

(d)   Abusive debt collection practices are carried on to a substantial extent in interstate commerce and through means and instrumentalities of such commerce. Even where abusive debt collection practices are purely intrastate in character, they nevertheless directly affect interstate commerce.

(e)   It is the purpose of this title to eliminate abusive debt collection practices by debt collectors, to insure that those debt collectors who refrain from using abusive debt collection practices are not competitively disadvantaged, and to promote consistent State action to protect consumers against debt collection abuses.

§ 803. Definitions [15 USC 1692a]

As used in this title—

(1) The term "Commission" means the Federal Trade Commission.

(2) The term "communication" means the conveying of information regarding a debt directly or indirectly to any person through any medium.

(3) The term "consumer" means any natural person obligated or allegedly obligated to pay any debt.

(4) The term "creditor" means any person who offers or extends credit creating a debt or to whom a debt is owed, but such term does not include any person to the extent that he receives an assignment or transfer of a debt in default solely for the purpose of facilitating collection of such debt for another.

(5) The term "debt" means any obligation or alleged obligation of a consumer to pay money arising out of a transaction in which the money, property, insurance or services which are the subject of the transaction are primarily for personal, family, or household purposes, whether or not such obligation has been reduced to judgment.

(6) The term "debt collector" means any person who uses any instrumentality of interstate commerce or the mails in any business the principal purpose of which is the collection of any debts, or who regularly collects or attempts to collect, directly or indirectly, debts owed or due or asserted to be owed or due another. Notwithstanding the exclusion provided by clause (F) of the last sentence of this paragraph, the term includes any creditor who, in the process of collecting his own debts, uses any name other than his own which would indicate that a third person is collecting or attempting to collect such debts. For the purpose of section 808(6), such term also includes any person who uses any instrumentality of interstate commerce or the

mails in any business the principal purpose of which is the enforcement of security interests. The term does not include—

(A)   any officer or employee of a creditor while, in the name of the creditor, collecting debts for such creditor;

(B)   any person while acting as a debt collector for another person, both of whom are related by common ownership or affiliated by corporate control, if the person acting as a debt collector does so only for persons to whom it is so related or affiliated and if the principal business of such person is not the collection of debts;

(C)   any officer or employee of the United States or any State to the extent that collecting or attempting to collect any debt is in the performance of his official duties;

(D)   any person while serving or attempting to serve legal process on any other person in connection with the judicial enforcement of any debt;

(E)   any nonprofit organization which, at the request of consumers, performs bona fide consumer credit counseling and assists consumers in the liquidation of their debts by receiving payments from such consumers and distributing such amounts to creditors; and

(F)   any person collecting or attempting to collect any debt owed or due or asserted to be owed or due another to the extent such activity (i) is incidental to a bona fide fiduciary obligation or a bona fide escrow arrangement; (ii) concerns a debt which was originated by such person; (iii) concerns a debt which was not in default at the time it was obtained by such person; or (iv) concerns a debt obtained by such person as a secured party in a commercial credit transaction involving the creditor.

(7)   The term "location information" means a consumer's place of abode and his telephone number at such place, or his place of employment.

(8)   The term "State" means any State, territory, or possession of the United States, the District of Columbia, the Commonwealth of Puerto Rico, or any political subdivision of any of the foregoing.

§ 804. Acquisition of location information [15 USC 1692b]

Any debt collector communicating with any person other than the consumer for the purpose of acquiring location information about the consumer shall—

(1) identify himself, state that he is confirming or correcting location information concerning the consumer, and, only if expressly requested, identify his employer;

(2) not state that such consumer owes any debt;

(3) not communicate with any such person more than once unless requested to do so by such person or unless the debt collector reasonably believes that the earlier response of such person is erroneous or incomplete and that such person now has correct or complete location information;

(4) not communicate by post card;

(5) not use any language or symbol on any envelope or in the contents of any communication effected by the mails or telegram that indicates that the debt collector is in the debt collection business or that the communication relates to the collection of a debt; and

(6) after the debt collector knows the consumer is represented by an attorney with regard to the subject debt and has knowledge of, or can readily ascertain, such attorney's name and address, not communicate with any person other than that attorney, unless

the attorney fails to respond within a reasonable period of time to the communication from the debt collector.

§ 805. Communication in connection with debt collection [15 USC 1692c]

(a) COMMUNICATION WITH THE CONSUMER GENERALLY. Without the prior consent of the consumer given directly to the debt collector or the express permission of a court of competent jurisdiction, a debt collector may not communicate with a consumer in connection with the collection of any debt—

    (1)   at any unusual time or place or a time or place known or which should be known to be inconvenient to the consumer. In the absence of knowledge of circumstances to the contrary, a debt collector shall assume that the convenient time for communicating with a consumer is after 8 o'clock antimeridian and before 9 o'clock postmeridian, local time at the consumer's location;

    (2)   if the debt collector knows the consumer is represented by an attorney with respect to such debt and has knowledge of, or can readily ascertain, such attorney's name and address, unless the attorney fails to respond within a reasonable period of time to a communication from the debt collector or unless the attorney consents to direct communication with the consumer; or

    (3)   at the consumer's place of employment if the debt collector knows or has reason to know that the consumer's employer prohibits the consumer from receiving such communication.

(b) COMMUNICATION WITH THIRD PARTIES. Except as provided in section 804, without the prior consent of the consumer given directly to the debt collector, or the express permission of a court of competent jurisdiction, or as reasonably necessary to effectuate a postjudgment judicial remedy, a debt collector may not communicate, in connection with the collection of any debt, with any person other than a consumer, his attorney, a consumer reporting agency if otherwise permitted by law, the creditor, the attorney of the creditor, or the attorney of the debt collector.

(c)　CEASING COMMUNICATION. If a consumer notifies a debt collector in writing that the consumer refuses to pay a debt or that the consumer wishes the debt collector to cease further communication with the consumer, the debt collector shall not communicate further with the consumer with respect to such debt, except—

(1)　to advise the consumer that the debt collector's further efforts are being terminated;

(2)　to notify the consumer that the debt collector or creditor may invoke specified remedies which are ordinarily invoked by such debt collector or creditor; or

(3)　where applicable, to notify the consumer that the debt collector or creditor intends to invoke a specified remedy.

　　　If such notice from the consumer is made by mail, notification shall be complete upon receipt.

(d)　For the purpose of this section, the term "consumer" includes the consumer's spouse, parent (if the consumer is a minor), guardian, executor, or administrator.

§ 806. Harassment or abuse [15 USC 1692d]

A debt collector may not engage in any conduct the natural consequence of which is to harass, oppress, or abuse any person in connection with the collection of a debt. Without limiting the general application of the foregoing, the following conduct is a violation of this section:

(1) The use or threat of use of violence or other criminal means to harm the physical person, reputation, or property of any person.

(2) The use of obscene or profane language or language the natural consequence of which is to abuse the hearer or reader.

(3) The publication of a list of consumers who allegedly refuse to pay debts, except to a consumer reporting agency or to persons meeting the requirements of section 603(f) or 604(3)1 of this Act.

(4) The advertisement for sale of any debt to coerce payment of the debt.

(5) Causing a telephone to ring or engaging any person in telephone conversation repeatedly or continuously with intent to annoy, abuse, or harass any person at the called number.

(6) Except as provided in section 804, the placement of telephone calls without meaningful disclosure of the caller's identity.

§ 807. False or misleading representations [15 USC 1962e]

A debt collector may not use any false, deceptive, or misleading representation or means in connection with the collection of any debt. Without limiting the general application of the foregoing, the following conduct is a violation of this section:

(1) The false representation or implication that the debt collector is vouched for, bonded by, or affiliated with the United States or any State, including the use of any badge, uniform, or facsimile thereof.

(2) The false representation of —

    (A) the character, amount, or legal status of any debt; or

    (B) any services rendered or compensation which may be lawfully received by any debt collector for the collection of a debt.

(3) The false representation or implication that any individual is an attorney or that any communication is from an attorney.

(4) The representation or implication that nonpayment of any debt will result in the arrest or imprisonment of any person or the seizure, garnishment, attachment, or sale of any property or wages of any person unless such action is lawful and the debt collector or creditor intends to take such action.

(5) The threat to take any action that cannot legally be taken or that is not intended to be taken.

(6) The false representation or implication that a sale, referral, or other transfer of any interest in a debt shall cause the consumer to —

(A) lose any claim or defense to payment of the debt; or

(B) become subject to any practice prohibited by this title.

(7) The false representation or implication that the consumer committed any crime or other conduct in order to disgrace the consumer.

(8) Communicating or threatening to communicate to any person credit information which is known or which should be known to be false, including the failure to communicate that a disputed debt is disputed.

(9) The use or distribution of any written communication which simulates or is falsely represented to be a document authorized, issued, or approved by any court, official, or agency of the United States or any State, or which creates a false impression as to its source, authorization, or approval.

(10) The use of any false representation or deceptive means to collect or attempt to collect any debt or to obtain information concerning a consumer.

(11) The failure to disclose in the initial written communication with the consumer and, in addition, if the initial communication with the consumer is oral, in that initial oral communication, that the debt collector is attempting to collect a debt and

that any information obtained will be used for that purpose, and the failure to disclose in subsequent communications that the communication is from a debt collector, except that this paragraph shall not apply to a formal pleading made in connection with a legal action.

(12) The false representation or implication that accounts have been turned over to innocent purchasers for value.

(13) The false representation or implication that documents are legal process.

(14) The use of any business, company, or organization name other than the true name of the debt collector's business, company, or organization.

(15) The false representation or implication that documents are not legal process forms or do not require action by the consumer.

(16) The false representation or implication that a debt collector operates or is employed by a consumer reporting agency as defined by section 603(f) of this Act.

§ 808. Unfair practices [15 USC 1692f]

A debt collector may not use unfair or unconscionable means to collect or attempt to collect any debt. Without limiting the general application of the foregoing, the following conduct is a violation of this section:

(1) The collection of any amount (including any interest, fee, charge, or expense incidental to the principal obligation) unless such amount is expressly authorized by the agreement creating the debt or permitted by law.

(2) The acceptance by a debt collector from any person of a check or other payment instrument postdated by more than five days unless such person is notified in writing of the debt collector's

intent to deposit such check or instrument not more than ten nor less than three business days prior to such deposit.

(3) The solicitation by a debt collector of any postdated check or other postdated payment instrument for the purpose of threatening or instituting criminal prosecution.

(4) Depositing or threatening to deposit any postdated check or other postdated payment instrument prior to the date on such check or instrument.

(5) Causing charges to be made to any person for communications by concealment of the true propose of the communication. Such charges include, but are not limited to, collect telephone calls and telegram fees.

(6) Taking or threatening to take any nonjudicial action to effect dispossession or disablement of property if —

    (A)   there is no present right to possession of the property claimed as collateral through an enforceable security interest;

    (B)   there is no present intention to take possession of the property; or

    (C)   the property is exempt by law from such dispossession or disablement.

(7) Communicating with a consumer regarding a debt by post card.

(8) Using any language or symbol, other than the debt collector's address, on any envelope when communicating with a con sumer by use of the mails or by telegram, except that a debt collector may use his business name if such name does not indicate that he is in the debt collection business.

§ 809. Validation of debts [15 USC 1692g]

    (a)   Within five days after the initial communication with a consumer in connection with the collection of any debt, a debt collector shall, unless the following information is contained in the initial communication or the consumer has paid the debt, send the consumer a written notice containing—

(1)   the amount of the debt;

(2)   the name of the creditor to whom the debt is owed;

(3)   a statement that unless the consumer, within thirty days after receipt of the notice, disputes the validity of the debt, or any portion thereof, the debt will be assumed to be valid by the debt collector;

(4)   a statement that if the consumer notifies the debt collector in writing within the thirty-day period that the debt, or any portion thereof, is disputed, the debt collector will obtain verification of the debt or a copy of a judgment against the consumer and a copy of such verification or judgment will be mailed to the consumer by the debt collector; and

(5)   a statement that, upon the consumer's written request within the thirty-day period, the debt collector will provide the consumer with the name and address of the original creditor, if different from the current creditor.

(b) If the consumer notifies the debt collector in writing within the thirty-day period described in subsection (a) that the debt, or any portion thereof, is disputed, or that the consumer requests the name and address of the original creditor, the debt collector shall cease collection of the debt, or any disputed portion thereof, until the debt collector obtains verification of the debt or any copy of a judgment, or the name and address of the original creditor, and a copy of such verification or judgment, or name and address of the original creditor, is mailed to the consumer by the debt collector.

(c)   The failure of a consumer to dispute the validity of a debt under this section may not be construed by any court as an admission of liability by the consumer.

§ 810. Multiple debts [15 USC 1692h]

If any consumer owes multiple debts and makes any single payment to any debt collector with respect to such debts, such debt collector may not apply such payment to any debt which is disputed by the consumer and, where applicable, shall apply such payment in accordance with the consumer's directions.

§ 811. Legal actions by debt collectors [15 USC 1692i]

(a)   Any debt collector who brings any legal action on a debt against any consumer shall—

(1)   in the case of an action to enforce an interest in real property securing the consumer's obligation, bring such action only in a judicial district or similar legal entity in which such real property is located; or

(2)   in the case of an action not described in paragraph (1), bring such action only in the judicial district or similar legal entity—

(A)   in which such consumer signed the contract sued upon; or

(B)   in which such consumer resides at the commencement of the action.

(b)   Nothing in this title shall be construed to authorize the bringing of legal actions by debt collectors.

§ 812. Furnishing certain deceptive forms [15 USC 1692j]

(a)   It is unlawful to design, compile, and furnish any form knowing that such form would be used to create the false belief in a consumer that a person other than the creditor of such consumer is participating in the collection of or in an attempt to collect a debt such consumer allegedly owes such creditor, when in fact such person is not so participating.

(b) Any person who violates this section shall be liable to the same extent and in the same manner as a debt collector is liable under section 813 for failure to comply with a provision of this title.

§ 813. Civil liability [15 USC 1692k]

(a) Except as otherwise provided by this section, any debt collector who fails to comply with any provision of this title with respect to any person is liable to such person in an amount equal to the sum of—

(1) any actual damage sustained by such person as a result of such failure;

(2) (A) in the case of any action by an individual, such additional damages as the court may allow, but not exceeding $1,000; or

(B) in the case of a class action, (i) such amount for each named plaintiff as could be recovered under subparagraph (A), and (ii) such amount as the court may allow for all other class members, without regard to a minimum individual recovery, not to exceed the lesser of $500,000 or 1 per centum of the net worth of the debt collector; and

(3) in the case of any successful action to enforce the foregoing liability, the costs of the action, together with a reasonable attorney's fee as determined by the court. On a finding by the court that an action under this section was brought in bad faith and for the purpose of harassment, the court may award to the defendant attorney's fees reasonable in relation to the work expended and costs.

(b) In determining the amount of liability in any action under subsection (a), the court shall consider, among other relevant factors—

  (1)   in any individual action under subsection (a)(2)(A), the frequency and persistence of noncompliance by the debt collector, the nature of such noncompliance, and the extent to which such noncompliance was intentional; or

  (2)   in any class action under subsection (a)(2)(B), the frequency and persistence of noncompliance by the debt collector, the nature of such noncompliance, the resources of the debt collector, the number of persons adversely affected, and the extent to which the debt collector's noncompliance was intentional.

(c) A debt collector may not be held liable in any action brought under this title if the debt collector shows by a preponderance of evidence that the violation was not intentional and resulted from a bona fide error notwithstanding the maintenance of procedures reasonably adapted to avoid any such error.

(d) An action to enforce any liability created by this title may be brought in any appropriate United States district court without regard to the amount in controversy, or in any other court of competent jurisdiction, within one year from the date on which the violation occurs.

(e) No provision of this section imposing any liability shall apply to any act done or omitted in good faith in conformity with any advisory opinion of the Commission, notwithstanding that after such act or omission has occurred, such opinion is amended, rescinded, or determined by judicial or other authority to be invalid for any reason.

§ 814. Administrative enforcement [15 USC 1692l]

(a) Compliance with this title shall be enforced by the Commission, except to the extend that enforcement of the requirements imposed under this title is specifically committed to another agency under subsection (b). For purpose of the exercise by the Commission of its functions and powers under the Federal Trade Commission Act, a violation of this title shall be deemed an unfair or deceptive act or practice in violation of that Act. All of the functions and powers of the Commission under the Federal Trade Commission Act are available to the Commission to enforce compliance by any person with this title, irrespective of whether that person is engaged in commerce or meets any other jurisdictional tests in the Federal Trade Commission Act, including the power to enforce the provisions of this title in the same manner as if the violation had been a violation of a Federal Trade Commission trade regulation rule.

(b) Compliance with any requirements imposed under this title shall be enforced under—

    (1) section 8 of the Federal Deposit Insurance Act, in the case of—

        (A) national banks, by the Comptroller of the Currency;

        (B) member banks of the Federal Reserve System (other than national banks), by the Federal Reserve Board; and

        (C) banks the deposits or accounts of which are insured by the Federal Deposit Insurance Corporation (other than members of the Federal Reserve System), by the Board of Directors of the Federal Deposit Insurance Corporation;

(2)   section 5(d) of the Home Owners Loan Act of 1933, section 407 of the National Housing Act, and sections 6(i) and 17 of the Federal Home Loan Bank Act, by the Federal Home Loan Bank Board (acting directing or through the Federal Savings and Loan Insurance Corporation), in the case of any institution subject to any of those provisions;

(3)   the Federal Credit Union Act, by the Administrator of the National Credit Union Administration with respect to any Federal credit union;

(4)   subtitle IV of Title 49, by the Interstate Commerce Commission with respect to any common carrier subject to such subtitle;

(5)   the Federal Aviation Act of 1958, by the Secretary of Transportation with respect to any air carrier or any foreign air carrier subject to that Act; and

(6)   the Packers and Stockyards Act, 1921 (except as provided in section 406 of that Act), by the Secretary of Agriculture with respect to any activities subject to that Act.

(c)   For the purpose of the exercise by any agency referred to in subsection (b) of its powers under any Act referred to in that subsection, a violation of any requirement imposed under this title shall be deemed to be a violation of a requirement imposed under that Act. In addition to its powers under any provision of law specifically referred to in subsection (b), each of the agencies referred to in that subsection may exercise, for the purpose of enforcing compliance with any requirement imposed under this title any other authority conferred on it by law, except as provided in subsection (d).

(d)   Neither the Commission nor any other agency referred to in subsection (b) may promulgate trade regulation rules or other regulations with respect to the collection of debts by debt collectors as defined in this title.

§ 815. Reports to Congress by the Commission [15 USC 1692m]

(a) Not later than one year after the effective date of this title and at one-year intervals thereafter, the Commission shall make reports to the Congress concerning the administration of its functions under this title, including such recommendations as the Commission deems necessary or appropriate. In addition, each report of the Commission shall include its assessment of the extent to which compliance with this title is being achieved and a summary of the enforcement actions taken by the Commission under section 814 of this title.

(b) In the exercise of its functions under this title, the Commission may obtain upon request the views of any other Federal agency which exercises enforcement functions under section 814 of this title.

§ 816. Relation to State laws [15 USC 1692n]

This title does not annul, alter, or affect, or exempt any person subject to the provisions of this title from complying with the laws of any State with respect to debt collection practices, except to the extent that those laws are inconsistent with any provision of this title, and then only to the extent of the inconsistency. For purposes of this section, a State law is not inconsistent with this title if the protection such law affords any consumer is greater than the protection provided by this title.

§ 817. Exemption for State regulation [15 USC 1692o]

The Commission shall by regulation exempt from the requirements of this title any class of debt collection practices within any State if the Commission determines that under the law of that State that class of debt collection practices is subject to requirements substantially similar to those imposed by this title, and that there is adequate provision for enforcement.

§ 818. Effective date [15 USC 1692 note]

This title takes effect upon the expiration of six months after the date of its enactment, but section 809 shall apply only with respect to debts for which the initial attempt to collect occurs after such effective date.

Approved September 20, 1977

ENDNOTES

1. So in original; however, should read "604(a)(3)."

LEGISLATIVE HISTORY:

Public Law 95-109 [H.R. 5294]

HOUSE REPORT No. 95-131 (Comm. on Banking, Finance, and Urban Affairs).

SENATE REPORT No. 95-382 (Comm. on Banking, Housing, and Urban Affairs).

CONGRESSIONAL RECORD, Vol. 123 (1977):

Apr. 4, considered and passed House.

Aug. 5, considered and passed Senate, amended.

Sept. 8, House agreed to Senate amendment.

WEEKLY COMPILATION OF PRESIDENTIAL DOCUMENTS, Vol. 13, No. 39:

Sept. 20, Presidential statement.

AMENDMENTS:

SECTION 621, SUBSECTIONS (b)(3), (b)(4) and (b)(5) were amended to transfer certain administrative enforcement responsibilities, pursuant to Pub. L. 95-473, § 3(b), Oct. 17, 1978. 92 Stat. 166; Pub. L. 95-630, Title V. § 501, November 10, 1978, 92 Stat. 3680; Pub. L. 98-443, § 9(h), Oct. 4, 1984, 98 Stat. 708.

SECTION 803, SUBSECTION (6), defining "debt collector," was amended to repeal the attorney at law exemption at former Section

(6)(F) and to redesignate Section 803(6)(G) pursuant to Pub. L. 99-361, July 9, 1986, 100 Stat. 768. For legislative history, *see* H.R. 237, HOUSE REPORT No. 99-405 (Comm. on Banking, Finance and Urban Affairs). CONGRESSIONAL RECORD: Vol. 131 (1985): Dec. 2, considered and passed House. Vol. 132 (1986): June 26, considered and passed Senate.

SECTION 807, SUBSECTION (11), was amended to affect when debt collectors must state (a) that they are attempting to collect a debt and (b) that information obtained will be used for that purpose, pursuant to Pub. L. 104-208 § 2305, 110 Stat. 3009 (Sept. 30, 1996).

Appendix M—The Electronic Fund Transfer Act

Sec. 1693. Congressional findings and declaration of purpose

❖ (a) Rights and liabilities undefined The Congress finds that the use of electronic systems to transfer funds provides the potential for substantial benefits to consumers. However, due to the unique characteristics of such systems, the application of existing consumer protection legislation is unclear, leaving the rights and liabilities of consumers, financial institutions, and intermediaries in electronic fund transfers undefined.

❖ (b) Purposes It is the purpose of this subchapter to provide a basic framework establishing the rights, liabilities, and responsibilities of participants in electronic fund transfer systems. The primary objective of this subchapter, however, is the provision of individual consumer rights.

Appendix N—Consumer Protection Act

CHAPTER 41—CONSUMER CREDIT PROTECTION

SUBCHAPTER I—CONSUMER CREDIT COST DISCLOSURE

PART A—GENERAL PROVISIONS

§ 1605. Determination of finance charge.

    (a)   "Finance charge" defined.

    (b)   Life, accident, or health insurance premiums included in finance charge.

    (c)   Property damage and liability insurance premiums included in finance charge.

    (d)   Items exempted from computation of finance charge in all credit transactions.

    (e)   Items exempted from computation of finance charge in extensions of credit secured by an interest in real property.

    (f)   Tolerances for accuracy.

§ 1606. Determination of annual percentage rate.

    (a)   "Annual percentage rate" defined.

    (b)   Computation of rate of finance charges for balances within a specified range.

    (c)   Allowable tolerances for purposes of compliance with disclosure requirements.

    (d)   Use of rate tables or charts having allowable variance from determined rates.

    (e)   Authorization of tolerances in determining annual percentage rates.

§ 1607. Administrative enforcement.

    (a)   Enforcing agencies.

    (b)   Violations of this subchapter deemed violations of pre-existing statutory requirements; additional agency powers.

    (c)   Federal Trade Commission as overall enforcing agency.

    (d)   Rules and regulations.

    (e)   Adjustment of finance charges; procedures applicable, coverage, criteria, etc.

§ 1608. Views of other agencies.

§ 1609. Repealed.

§ 1610. Effect on other laws.

    (a)   Inconsistent provisions; procedures applicable for determination.

    (b)   State credit charge statutes.

    (c)   Disclosure as evidence.

    (d)   Contract or other obligations under State or Federal law.

    (e)   Certain credit and charge card application and solicitation disclosure provisions.

§ 1611. Criminal liability for willful and knowing violation.

§ 1612. Effect on government agencies.

    (a)   Consultation requirements respecting compliance of credit instruments issued to articipating creditor.

    (b)   Inapplicability of Federal civil or criminal penalties to Federal, State, and local agencies.

    (c)   Inapplicability of Federal civil or criminal penalties to participating creditor where violating instrument issued by United States.

    (d)   Applicability of State penalties to violations by participating creditor.

§ 1613. Annual reports to Congress by Board.

§ 1614. Repealed.

§ 1615. Prohibition on use of "Rule of 78's" in connection with mortgage refinancings and other consumer loans.

    (a)   Prompt refund of unearned interest required.

    (b)   Use of "Rule of 78's" prohibited.

    (c)   Statement of prepayment amount.

    (d)   Definitions.

PART B—CREDIT TRANSACTIONS

§ 1631. Disclosure requirements.

(a)   Duty of creditor or lessor respecting one or more than one obligor.

(b)   Creditor or lessor required to make disclosure.

(c)   Estimates as satisfying statutory requirements; basis of disclosure for per diem interest.

(d)   Tolerances for numerical disclosures.

§ 1632. Form of disclosure; additional information.

(a)   Information clearly and conspicuously disclosed; "annual percentage rate" and "finance charge"; order of disclosures and use of different terminology.

(b)   Optional information by creditor or lessor.

(c)   Tabular format required for certain disclosures under section 1637(c).

§ 1633. Exemption for State-regulated transactions.

§ 1634. Effect of subsequent occurrence.

§ 1635. Right of rescission as to certain transactions.

(a)   Disclosure of obligor's right to rescind.

(b)   Return of money or property following rescission.

(c)   Rebuttable presumption of delivery of required disclosures.

(d)   Modification and waiver of rights.

(e)   Exempted transactions; reapplication of provisions.

(f)   Time limit for exercise of right.

(g)   Additional relief.

(h)   Limitation on rescission.

(i)   Rescission rights in foreclosure.

§ 1636. Repealed.

§ 1637. Open end consumer credit plans.

(a)   Required disclosures by creditor.

PART D—CREDIT BILLING

§ 1666. Correction of billing errors.

    (a)   Written notice by obligor to creditor; time for and contents of notice; procedure upon receipt of notice by creditor.

    (b)   Billing error.

    (c)   Action by creditor to collect amount or any part thereof regarded by obligor to be a billing error.

    (d)   Restricting or closing by creditor of account regarded by obligor to contain a billing error.

    (e)   Effect of noncompliance with requirements by creditor.

§ 1666a. Regulation of credit reports.

    (a)   Reports by creditor on obligor's failure to pay amount regarded as billing error.

    (b)   Reports by creditor on delinquent amounts in dispute; notification of obligor of parties notified of delinquency.

    (c)   Reports by creditor of subsequent resolution of delinquent amounts.

§ 1666b. Length of billing period in credit statement for imposition of finance charge; effect of failure of timely mailing or delivery of statement.

    (a)   Additional finance charge.

    (b)   Excusable cause.

§ 1666c. Prompt crediting of payments; imposition of finance charge.

§ 1666d. Treatment of credit balances.

§ 1666e. Notification of credit card issuer by seller of return of goods, etc., by obligor; credit for account of obligor.

§ 1666f. Inducements to cardholders by sellers of cash discounts for payments by cash, check or similar means; credit card

PART E—CONSUMER LEASES

SUBCHAPTER II—RESTRICTIONS ON GARNISHMENT

SUBCHAPTER II-A—CREDIT REPAIR ORGANIZATIONS

§ 1679. Findings and purposes.

    (a)   Findings.

    (b)   Purposes.

§ 1679a. Definitions.

§ 1679b. Prohibited practices.

    (a)   In general.

    (b)   Payment in advance.

§ 1679c. Disclosures.

    (a)   Disclosure required.

    (b)   Separate statement requirement.

    (c)   Retention of compliance records.

§ 1679d. Credit repair organizations contracts.

    (a)   Written contracts required.

    (b)   Terms and conditions of contract.

§ 1679e. Right to cancel contract.

    (a)   In general.

    (b)   Cancellation form and other information.

    (c)   Consumer copy of contract required.

§ 1679f. Noncompliance with this subchapter.

    (a)   Consumer waivers invalid.

    (b)   Attempt to obtain waiver.

    (c)   Contracts not in compliance.

§ 1679g. Civil liability.

    (a)   Liability established.

    (b)   Factors to be considered in awarding punitive damages.

§ 1679h. Administrative enforcement.

    (a)   In general.

§ 1681d. Disclosure of investigative consumer reports.

 (a) Disclosure of fact of preparation.

 (b) Disclosure on request of nature and scope of investigation.

 (c) Limitation on liability upon showing of reasonable procedures for compliance with provisions.

 (d) Prohibitions.

§ 1681e. Compliance procedures.

 (a) Identity and purposes of credit users.

 (b) Accuracy of report.

 (c) Disclosure of consumer reports by users allowed.

 (d) Notice to users and furnishers of information.

 (e) Procurement of consumer report for resale.

§ 1681f. Disclosures to governmental agencies.

§ 1681g. Disclosures to consumers.

 (a) Information on file; sources; report recipients.

 (b) Exempt information.

 (c) Summary of rights required to be included with disclosure.

§ 1681h. Conditions and form of disclosure to consumers.

 (a) In general.

 (b) Other forms of disclosure.

 (c) Trained personnel.

 (d) Persons accompanying consumer.

 (e) Limitation of liability.

§ 1681i. Procedure in case of disputed accuracy.

 (a) Reinvestigations of disputed information.

 (b) Statement of dispute.

 (c) Notification of consumer dispute in subsequent consumer reports.

 (d) Notification of deletion of disputed information.

SUBCHAPTER IV—EQUAL CREDIT OPPORTUNITY

(c)   State laws prohibiting separate extension of consumer credit to husband and wife.

(d)   Combining credit accounts of husband and wife with same creditor to determine permissible finance charges or loan ceilings under Federal or State laws.

(e)   Election of remedies under subchapter or State law; nature of relief determining applicability.

(f)   Compliance with inconsistent State laws; determination of inconsistency.

(g)   Exemption by regulation of credit transactions covered by State law; failure to comply with State law.

§ 1691e. Civil liability.

(a)   Individual or class action for actual damages.

(b)   Recovery of punitive damages in individual and class action for actual damages; exemptions; maximum amount of punitive damages in individual actions; limitation on total recovery in class actions; factors determining amount of award.

(c)   Action for equitable and declaratory relief.

(d)   Recovery of costs and attorney fees.

(e)   Good faith compliance with rule, regulation, or interpretation of Board or interpretation or approval by an official or employee of Federal Reserve System duly authorized by Board.

(f)   Jurisdiction of courts; time for maintenance of action; exceptions.

(g)   Request by responsible enforcement agency to Attorney General for civil action.

(h)   Authority for Attorney General to bring civil action; jurisdiction.

Appendix O—Electronic Communications Privacy Act of 1986

UNITED STATES CODE
TITLE 18. CRIMES AND CRIMINAL PROCEDURE
PART I—CRIMES
CHAPTER 119—WIRE AND ELECTRONIC COMMUNICA-
TIONS INTERCEPTION AND
INTERCEPTION OF ORAL COMMUNICATIONS

_____Sec. 2510. Definitions

As used in this chapter—

(1) "wire communication" means any aural transfer made in whole
or in part through the use of facilities for the transmission of
communications by the aid of wire, cable, or other like connection between the point of origin and the point of reception
(including the use of such connection in a switching station)
furnished or operated by any person engaged in providing or
operating such facilities for the transmission of interstate or foreign communications for communications affecting interstate
or foreign commerce and such term includes any electronic
storage of such communication;

(2) "oral communication" means any oral communication uttered
by a person exhibiting an expectation that such communication
is not subject to interception under circumstances justifying

305

such expectation, but such term does not include any electronic communication;

(3) "State" means any State of the United States, the District of Columbia, the Commonwealth of Puerto Rico, and any territory or possession of the United States;

(4) "intercept" means the aural or other acquisition of the contents of any wire, electronic, or oral communication through the use of any electronic, mechanical, or other device;

(5) "electronic, mechanical, or other device" means any device or apparatus which can be used to intercept a wire, oral, or electronic communication other than—

    (a)   any telephone or telegraph instrument, equipment or facility, or any component thereof, (I) furnished to the subscriber or user by a provider of wire or electronic communication service in the ordinary course of its business and being used by the subscriber or user in the ordinary course of its business or furnished by such subscriber or user for connection to the facilities of such service and used in the ordinary course of its business; or (ii) being used by a provider of wire or electronic communication service in the ordinary course of its business, or by an investigative or law enforcement officer in the ordinary course of his duties;

    (b)   a hearing aid or similar device being used to correct subnormal hearing to not better than normal;

(6) "person" means any employee, or agent of the United States or any State or political subdivision thereof, and any individual, partnership, association, joint stock company, trust, or corporation;

(7) "Investigative or law enforcement officer" means any officer of the United States or of a State or political subdivision thereof, who is empowered by law to conduct investigations of or to

make arrests for offenses enumerated in this chapter, and any attorney authorized by law to prosecute or participate in the prosecution of such offenses;

(8) "contents", when used with respect to any wire, oral, or electronic communication, includes any information concerning the substance, purport, or meaning of that communication;

(9) "Judge of competent jurisdiction" means—

(a) a judge of a United States district court or a United States court of appeals; and

(b) a judge of any court of general criminal jurisdiction of a State who is authorized by a statute of that State to enter orders authorizing interceptions of wire, oral, or electronic communications;

(10) "communication common carrier" shall have the same meaning which is given the term "common carrier" by section 153(h) of title 47 of the United States Code;

(11) "aggrieved person" means a person who was a party to any intercepted wire, oral, or electronic communication or a person against whom the interception was directed;

(12) "electronic communication" means any transfer of signs, signals, writing, images, sounds, data, or intelligence of any nature transmitted in whole or in part by a wire, radio, electromagnetic, photoelectronic or photooptical system that affects interstate or foreign commerce, but does not include—

(A) any wire or oral communication;

(B) any communication made through a tone-only paging device; or

(C) any communication from a tracking device (as defined in section 3117 of this title);

(13) "user" means any person or entity who—

    (A)   uses an electronic communication service; and

    (B)   is duly authorized by the provider of such service to engage in such use;

(14) "electronic communications system" means any wire, radio, electromagnetic, photooptical or photoelectronic facilities for the transmission of electronic communications, and any computer facilities or related electronic equipment for the electronic storage of such communications;

(15) "electronic communication service" means any service which provides to users thereof the ability to send or receive wire or electronic communications;

(16) "readily accessible to the general public" means, with respect to a radio communication, that such communication is not—

    (A)   scrambled or encrypted:

    (B)   transmitted using modulation techniques whose essential parameters have been withheld from the public with the intention of preserving the privacy of such communication;

    (C)   carried on a subcarrier or other signal subsidiary to a radio transmission;

    (D)   transmitted over a communication system provided by a common carrier, unless the communication is a tone only paging system communication;

    (E)   transmitted on frequencies allocated under part 25, subpart D, E, or F of part 74, or part 94 of the Rules of the Federal Communications Commission, unless, in the case of a communication transmitted on a frequency allocated under part 74 that is not exclusively allocated to broadcast auxiliary services, the communication is a two-way voice communication by radio; or

    (F)   an electronic communication;

(17) "electronic storage" means—

- (A) any temporary, intermediate storage of a wire or electronic communication incidental to the electronic transmission thereof; and

- (B) any storage of such communication by an electronic communication service for purposes of backup protection of such communication; and

(18) "aural transfer" means a transfer containing the human voice at any point between and including the point of origin and the point of reception.

*   *   *

Sec. 2511. Interception and disclosure of wire, oral, or electronic communications prohibited

(1) Except as otherwise specifically provided in this chapter any person who—

- (a) intentionally intercepts, endeavors to intercept, or procures any other person to intercept or endeavor to intercept, any wire, oral, or electronic communication;

- (b) intentionally uses, endeavors to use, or procures any other person to use or endeavor to use any electronic, mechanical, or other device to intercept any oral communication when—

  - (i) such device is affixed to, or otherwise transmits a signal through, a wire, cable, or other like connection used in wire communication; or

  - (ii) such device transmits communications by radio, or interferes with the transmission of such communication; or

(iii)   such person knows, or has reason to know, that such device or any component thereof has been sent through the mail or transported in interstate or foreign commerce; or

(iv)   such use or endeavor to use (A) takes place on the premises of any business or other commercial establishment the operations of which affect interstate or foreign commerce; or (B) obtains or is for the purpose of obtaining information relating to the operations of any business or other commercial establishment the operations of which affect interstate or foreign commerce; or

(v)   such person acts in the District of Columbia, the Commonwealth of Puerto Rico, or any territory or possession of the United States;

(c)   intentionally discloses, or endeavors to disclose, to any other person the contents of any wire, oral, or electronic communication, knowing or having reason to know that the information was obtained through the interception of a wire, oral, or electronic communication in violation of this subsection;

(d)   intentionally uses, or endeavors to use, the contents of any wire, oral, or electronic communication, knowing or having reason to know that the information was obtained through the interception of a wire, oral, or electronic communication in violation of this subsection; or

(e)   (i) intentionally discloses, or endeavors to disclose, to any other person the contents of any wire, oral, or electronic communication, intercepted by means authorized by sections 2511(2)(A)(ii), 2511(b)-(c), 2511(e), 2516, and

2518 of this subchapter, (ii) knowing or having reason to know that the information was obtained through the interception of such a communication in connection with a criminal investigation, (iii) having obtained or received the information in connection with a criminal investigation, and (iv) with intent to improperly obstruct, impede, or interfere with a duly authorized criminal investigation, shall be punished as provided in subsection (4) or shall be subject to suit as provided in subsection (5).

(2) (a) (i) It shall not be unlawful under this chapter for an operator of a switchboard, or on officer, employee, or agent of a provider of wire or electronic communication service, whose facilities are used in the transmission of a wire or electronic communication, to intercept, disclose, or use that communication in the normal course of his employment while engaged in any activity which is a necessary incident to the rendition of his service or to the protection of the rights or property of the provider of that service, except that a provider of wire communication service to the public shall not utilize service observing or random monitoring except for mechanical or service quality control checks.

(ii) Notwithstanding any other law, providers of wire or electronic communication service, their officers, employees, and agents, landlords, custodians, or other persons, are authorized to provide information, facilities, or technical assistance to persons authorized by law to intercept wire, oral, or electronic communications or to conduct electronic surveillance, as defined in section 101 of the Foreign Intelligence Surveillance Act of 1978, if such provider, its officers, employees, or agents, landlord, custodian, or other specified person, has been provided with—

(A)   a court order directing such assistance signed by the authorizing judge, or

(B)   a certification in writing by a person specified in section 2518(7) of this title or the Attorney General of the United States that no warrant or court order is required by law, that all statutory requirements have been met, and that the specified assistance is required, setting forth the period of time during which the provision of the information, facilities, or technical assistance is authorized and specifying the information, facilities, or technical assistance required. No provider of wire or electronic communication service, officer, employee, or agent thereof, or landlord, custodian, or other specified person shall disclose the existence of any interception or surveillance or the device used to accomplish the interception or surveillance with respect to which the person has been furnished a court order or certification under this chapter, except as may otherwise be required by legal process and then only after prior notification to the Attorney General or to the principal prosecuting attorney of a State or any political subdivision of a State, as may be appropriate. Any such disclosure, shall render such person liable for the civil damages provided for in section 2520. No cause of action shall lie in any court against any provider of wire or electronic communication service, its officers, employees, or agents, landlord, custodian, or other specified person for providing information, facilities, or assistance in accordance with the terms of a court order or certification under this chapter.

(b) It shall not be unlawful under this chapter for an officer, employee, or agent of the Federal Communications Commission, in the normal course of his employment and in discharge of the monitoring responsibilities exercised by the Commission in the enforcement of chapter 5 of title 47 of the United States Code, to intercept a wire or electronic communication, or oral communication transmitted by radio, or to disclose or use the information thereby obtained.

(c) It shall not be unlawful under this chapter for a person acting under color of law to intercept a wire, oral, or electronic communication, where such person is a party to the communication or one of the parties to the communication has given prior consent to such interception.

(d)　　It shall not be unlawful under this chapter for a person not acting under color of law to intercept a wire, oral, or electronic communication where such person is a party to the communication or where one of the parties to the communication has given prior consent to such interception unless such communication is intercepted for the purpose of committing any criminal or tortious act in violation of the Constitution or laws of the United States or of any State.

(e)　　Notwithstanding any other provision of this title or section 705 or 706 of the Communications Act of 1934, it shall not be unlawful for an officer, employee, or agent of the United States in the normal course of his official duty to conduct electronic surveillance, as defined in section 101 of the Foreign Intelligence Surveillance Act of 1978, as authorized by that Act.

(f)　　Nothing contained in this chapter or chapter 121, or section 705 of the Communications Act of 1934, shall be deemed to affect the acquisition by the United States Government of foreign intelligence information from international or foreign communications, or foreign intelligence activities conducted in accordance with otherwise applicable Federal law involving a foreign electronic communications system, utilizing a means other than electronic surveillance as defined in section 101 of the Foreign Intelligence Surveillance Act of 1978, and procedures in this chapter and the Foreign Intelligence Surveillance Act of 1978 shall be the exclusive means by which electronic surveillance, as defined in section 101 of such Act, and the interception of domestic wire and oral communications may be conducted.

(g)   It shall not be unlawful under this chapter or chapter 121 of this title for any person—

(i)   to intercept or access an electronic communication made through an electronic communication system that is configured so that such electronic communication is readily accessible to the general public;

(ii)   to intercept any radio communication which is transmitted—

(I)   by any station for the use of the general public, or that relates to ships, aircraft, vehicles, or persons in distress;

(II)   by any governmental, law enforcement, civil defense, private land mobile, or public safety communications system, including police and fire, readily accessible to the general public;

(III)   by a station operating on an authorized frequency within the bands allocated to the amateur, citizens band, or general mobile radio services; or

(IV)   by any marine or aeronautical communications system;

(iii)   to engage in any conduct which—

(I)   is prohibited by section 633 of the Communications Act of 1934; or

(II)   is excepted from the application of section 705(a) of the Communications Act of 1934 by section 705(b) of that Act;

(iv)   to intercept any wire or electronic communication the transmission of which is causing harmful interference to any lawfully operating station or consumer electronic equipment, to the extent necessary to identify the source of such interference; or

(v) for other users of the same frequency to intercept any radio communication made through a system that utilizes frequencies monitored by individuals engaged in the provision or the use of such system, if such communication is not scrambled or encrypted.

(h) It shall not be unlawful under this chapter—

(i) to use a pen register or a trap and trace device (as those terms are defined for the purposes of chapter 206 (relating to pen registers and trap and trace devices) of this title); or

(ii) for a provider of electronic communication service to record the fact that a wire or electronic communication was initiated or completed in order to protect such provider, another provider furnishing service toward the completion of the wire or electronic communication, or a user of that service, from fraudulent, unlawful or abusive use of such service.

(3) (a) Except as provided in paragraph (b) of this subsection, a person or entity providing an electronic communication service to the public shall not intentionally divulge the contents of any communication (other than one to such person or entity, or an agent thereof) while in transmission on that service to any person or entity other than an addressee or intended recipient of such communication or an agent of such addressee or intended recipient.

(b) A person or entity providing electronic communication service to the public may divulge the contents of any such communication—

 (i) as otherwise authorized in section 2511(2)(a) or 2517 of this title;

 (ii) with the lawful consent of the originator or any addressee or intended recipient of such |communication;

 (iii) to a person employed or authorized, or whose facilities are used, to forward such communication to its destination; or

 (iv) which were inadvertently obtained by the service provider and which appear to pertain to the commission of a crime, if such divulgence is made to a law enforcement agency.

(4) (a) Except as provided in paragraph (b) of this subsection or in subsection (5), whoever violates subsection (1) of this section shall be fined under this title or imprisoned not more than five years, or both.

 (b) If the offense is a first offense under paragraph (a) of this subsection and is not for a tortious or illegal purpose or for purposes of direct or indirect commercial advantage or private commercial gain, and the wire or electronic communication with respect to which the offense under paragraph (a) is a radio communication that is not scrambled, encrypted, or transmitted using modulation techniques the essential parameters of which have been withheld from the public with the intention of preserving the privacy of such communication, then—

(i)   if the communication is not the radio portion of a cellular telephone communication, a cordless telephone communication that is transmitted between the cordless telephone handset and the base unit, a public land mobile radio service communication or a paging service communication, and the conduct is not that described in subsection (5), the offender shall be fined under this title or imprisoned not more than one year, or both; and

(ii)   if the communication is the radio portion of a cellular telephone communication, a cordless telephone communication that is transmitted between the cordless telephone handset and the base unit, a public land mobile radio service communication or a paging service communication, the offender shall be fined under this title.

(c)   Conduct otherwise an offense under this subsection that consists of or relates to the interception of a satellite transmission that is not encrypted or scrambled and that is transmitted—

(i)   to a broadcasting station for purposes of retransmission to the general public; or

(ii)   as an audio subcarrier intended for redistribution to facilities open to the public, but not including data transmissions or telephone calls, is not an offense under this subsection unless the conduct is for the purposes of direct or indirect commercial advantage or private financial gain.

(5) (a) (i) If the communication is—

(A) a private satellite video communication that is not scrambled or encrypted and the conduct in violation of this chapter is the private viewing of that communication and is not for a tortious or illegal purpose or for purposes of direct or indirect commercial advantage or private commercial gain; or

(B) a radio communication that is transmitted on frequencies allocated under subpart D of part 74 of the rules of the Federal Communications Commission that is not scrambled or encrypted and the conduct in violation of this chapter is not for a tortious or illegal purpose or for purposes of direct or indirect commercial advantage or private commercial gain, then the person who engages in such conduct shall be subject to suit by the Federal Government in a court of competent jurisdiction.

(ii) In an action under this subsection—

(A) if the violation of this chapter is a first offense for the person under paragraph (a) of subsection (4) and such person has not been found liable in a civil action under section 2520 of this title, the Federal Government shall be entitled to appropriate injunctive relief; and

(B)   if the violation of this chapter is a second or subsequent offense under paragraph (a) of subsection (4) or such person has been found liable in any prior civil action under section 2520, the person shall be subject to a mandatory $500 civil fine.

(b)   The court may use any means within its authority to enforce an injunction issued under paragraph (ii)(A), and shall impose a civil fine of not less than $500 for each violation of such an injunction.

*   *   *

Sec. 2512. Manufacture, distribution, possession, and advertising of wire, oral, or electronic communication intercepting devices prohibited. (TEXT OF STATUTE OMITTED)

*   *   *

Sec. 2513. Confiscation of wire, oral, or electronic communication intercepting devices. (TEXT OF STATUTE OMITTED)

*   *   *

Sec. 2514. (REPEALED)

*   *   *

Sec. 2515. Prohibition of use as evidence of intercepted wire or oral communications

Whenever any wire or oral communication has been intercepted, no part of the contents of such communication and no evidence derived therefrom may be received in evidence in any trial, hearing, or other proceeding in or before any court, grand jury, department, officer, agency, regulatory body, legislative committee, or other authority of the United States, a State, or a political subdivision thereof if the disclosure of that information would be in violation of this chapter.

*   *   *

Sec. 2516. Authorization for interception of wire, oral, or electronic communications. (TEXT OF STATUTE OMITTED)

*   *   *

Sec. 2517. Authorization for disclosure and use of intercepted wire, oral, or electronic communications. (TEXT OF STATUTE OMITTED)

*   *   *

Sec. 2518. Procedure for interception of wire, oral, or electronic communications. (TEXT OF STATUTE OMITTED)

*   *   *

Sec. 2519. Reports concerning intercepted wire, oral, or electronic communications. (TEXT OF STATUTE OMITTED)

*   *   *

Sec. 2520. Recovery of civil damages authorized.

(a) In general. Except as provided in section 2511(2)(a)(ii), any person whose wire, oral, or electronic communication is intercepted, disclosed, or intentionally used in violation of this chapter may in a civil action recover from the person or entity which engaged in that violation such relief as may be appropriate.

(b) Relief. In an action under this section, appropriate relief includes—

    (1) such preliminary and other equitable or declaratory relief as may be appropriate;

    (2) damages under subsection (c) and punitive damages in appropriate cases; and

    (3) a reasonable attorney's fee and other litigation costs reasonably incurred.

(c) Computation of damages.

    (1) In an action under this section, if the conduct in violation of this chapter is the private viewing of a private satellite video communication that is not scrambled or encrypted or if the communication is a radio communication that is transmitted on frequencies allocated under subpart D of part 74 of the rules of the Federal Communications Commission that is not scrambled or encrypted and the conduct is not for a tortious or illegal purpose or for purposes of direct or indirect commercial advantage or private commercial gain, then the court shall assess damages as follows:

    (A)   If the person who engaged in that conduct has not previously been enjoined under section 2511(5) and has not been found liable in a prior civil action under this section, the court shall assess the greater of the sum of actual damages suffered by the plaintiff, or statutory damages of not less than $50 and not more than $500.

    (B)   If, on one prior occasion, the person who engaged in that conduct has been enjoined under section 2511(5) or has been found liable in a civil action under this section, the court shall assess the greater of the sum of actual damages suffered by the plaintiff, or statutory damages of not less than $100 and not more than $1000.

  (2)   In any other action under this section, the court may assess as damages whichever is the greater of

    (A)   the sum of the actual damages suffered by the plaintiff and any profits made by the violator as a result of the violation; or

    (B)   statutory damages of whichever is the greater of $100 a day for each day of violation or $10,000.

(d) Defense. A good faith reliance on—

  (1)   a court warrant or order, a grand jury subpoena, a legislative authorization, or a statutory authorization;

  (2)   a request of an investigative or law enforcement officer under section 2518(7) of this title; or

  (3)   a good faith determination that section 2511(3) of this title permitted the conduct complained of; is a complete defense against any civil or criminal action brought under this chapter or any other law.

(e) Limitation. A civil action under this section may not be commenced later than two years after the date upon which the claimant first has a reasonable opportunity to discover the violation.

*   *   *

Sec. 2521. Injunction against illegal interception. (TEXT OF STATUTE OMITTED)

*   *   *

Sec. 2522. Enforcement of the communications assistance for law enforcement act. (TEXT OF STATUTE OMITTED)

Appendix P—Children's Online Privacy Protection Act of 1998

(S 2326 IS)

To require the Federal Trade Commission to prescribe regulations to protect the privacy of personal information collected from and about children on the Internet, to provide greater parental control over the collection and use of that information, and for other purposes.

July 17, 1998

SECTION 1. SHORT TITLE.

This Act may be cited as the 'Children's Online Privacy Protection Act of 1998'.

SEC. 2. DEFINITIONS.

In this Act:

(1) CHILD—The term 'child' means an individual under the age of 16.

(2) CHILDREN- The term 'children' means more than 1 child.

(3) COMMERCIAL WEBSITE OPERATOR- The term 'commercial website operator' means any person operating a website on the World Wide Webs for commercial purposes, including any person offering products or services for sale though that website, involving commerce—

   (A) among the several States or with 1 or more foreign nations;

    (B)   in any territory of the United States or in the District of Columbia, or between any such territory—

        (i)   and another such territory; or

        (ii)   and any State or foreign nation; or

    (C)   between the District of Columbia and any State, territory, or foreign nation.

(4) COMMISSION- The term `Commission' means the Federal Trade Commission.

(5) DISCLOSURE- The term `disclosure' means, with respect to personal information—

    (A)   the release of information in identifiable form by a person to any other person for any purpose; or

    (B)   making publicly available information in identifiable form by any means including by a public posting, through the use of a computer on or through—

        (i)   a home page of a website;

        (ii)   a pen pal service;

        (iii)   an electronic mail service;

        (iv)   a message board; or

        (v)   a chat room.

(6) FEDERAL AGENCY—The term `Federal agency' means an agency, as that term is defined in section 551(1) of title 5, United States Code.

(7) INTERNET- The term `Internet' means the international computer network of both Federal and non-Federal interoperable packet switched data networks.

(8) PARENT- The term `parent' means a legal guardian, including a biological or adoptive parent.

(9) PERSONAL INFORMATION—The term 'personal information' means individually, identifiable information about an individual, including—

(A)   a first and last name;

(B)   a home or other physical address;

(C)   an e-mail address;

(D)   a telephone number;

(E)   a Social Security number; or

(F)   any other information that would facilitate or enable the physical or online locating and contacting of a specific individual, including information that is associated with an identifier described in this paragraph in such manner as to become identifiable to a specific individual.

(10) VERIFIABLE PARENTAL CONSENT- The term 'verifiable parental consent' means any reasonable effort (taking into consideration available technology) to ensure that a parent of a child authorizes the disclosure of personal information and subsequent use of that information before that information is collected from that child.

(11) WEBSITE DIRECTED TO CHILDREN—The term 'website directed to children'—

(A)   means a commercial website that is—

(i)   targeted to children;

(ii)   directed to children by reason of the subject matter, visual content, age of models, language, characters, tone, message, or any other similar characteristic of the website; or

(iii) used by a commercial website operator to knowingly collect information from children; and

(B)   includes any commercial website any portion of which is directed to children, as specified in subparagraph (A).

(12) PERSON—The term 'person' means any individual, partnership, corporation, trust, estate, cooperative, association, or other entity.

SEC. 3. REGULATION OF UNFAIR AND DECEPTIVE ACTS AND PRACTICES IN CONNECTION WITH THE COLLECTION AND USE OF PERSONAL INFORMATION FROM AND ABOUT CHILDREN ON THE INTERNET.

(a) REGULATIONS—

(1)   IN GENERAL- Not later than 1 year after the date of enactment of this Act, the Commission shall, in a manner consistent with section 553 of title 5, United States Code, prescribe regulations requiring commercial website operators to follow fair information practices in connection with the collection and use of personal information from children.

(2)   CONTENTS- The regulations issued under this subsection shall—

(A)   require that any website directed to children that collects personal information from children—

(i)   provide clear, prominent, understandable notice of the information collection and use practices of the website operator through the website;

(ii)   obtain verifiable parental consent for the collection, use, or disclosure of personal Information from children who are under the age of 13;

(iii)   use reasonable efforts to provide the parents with notice and an opportunity to prevent or curtail the collection or use of personal information collected from children over the age of 12 and under the age of 17;

(iv)   provide a parent—

    (I)   access to the personal information of the child of that parent collected by that website; and

    (II)   the opportunity to refuse to permit any further use or future collection of personal information referred to in subclause (I) and notice of that opportunity; and

(B)   require that the commercial website operator concerned establish and maintain reasonable procedures to ensure the confidentiality, security, accuracy, and integrity of personal information collected from children through the website.

(b) ENFORCEMENT—

(1)   TREATMENT OF REGULATIONS- A regulation prescribed under subsection (a) shall be treated as a rule defining an unfair or deceptive act or practice under section 18(a)(1)(B) of the Federal Trade Commission Act (15 U.S.C. 57a(a)(1)(B)).

(2)   ENFORCEMENT- Subject to section 6, a violation of a regulation prescribed under subsection (a) shall be treated as a violation of a rule defining an unfair or deceptive act or practice prescribed under section 18(a)(1)(B) of the Federal Trade Commission Act.

SEC. 4. SAFE HARBORS.

(a) IN GENERAL- In prescribing regulations under section 3, the Commission shall provide incentives for efforts of self-regulation by commercial website operators to implement the protections described in subsection (a) of that section.

(b) SAFE HARBORS- The incentives referred to in subsection (a) shall include provisions for ensuring that a person will be deemed to be in compliance with the requirements of the regulations under section 3 if that person applies guidelines that—

    (1) are issued by appropriate representatives of the computer industry; and

    (2) are approved by the Commission upon making a determination that the guidelines meet the requirements of the regulations issued under section 3.

SEC. 5. ACTIONS BY STATES.

(a) IN GENERAL—

    (1) CIVIL ACTIONS- In any case in which the attorney general of a State has reason to believe that an interest of the residents of that State has been or is threatened or adversely affected by the engagement of any person in a practice that violates any regulation of the Commission prescribed under section 3, the State, as parens patriae, may bring a civil action on behalf of the residents of the State in a district court of the United States of appropriate jurisdiction to—

        (A) enjoin that practice;

        (B) enforce compliance with the regulation;

        (C) obtain damage, restitution, or other compensation on behalf of residents of the State; or

        (D) obtain such other relief as the court may consider to be appropriate.

(2)   NOTICE-

    (A)   IN GENERAL- Before filing an action under paragraph (1), the attorney general of the State involved shall provide to the Commission—

        (i)   written notice of that action; and

        (ii)   a copy of the complaint for that action.

    (B)   EXEMPTION—

        (i)   IN GENERAL- Subparagraph (A) shall not apply with respect to the filing of an action by an attorney general of a State under this subsection, if the attorney general determines that it is not feasible to provide the notice described in that subparagraph before the filing of the action.

        (ii)   NOTIFICATION- In an action described in clause (i), the attorney general of a State shall provide notice and a copy of the complaint to the Commission at the same time as the attorney general files the action.

(b) INTERVENTION—

    (1)   IN GENERAL- On receiving notice under paragraph (2), the Commission shall have the right to intervene in the action that is the subject of the notice.

    (2)   EFFECT OF INTERVENTION- If the Commission intervenes in an action under subparagraph (A), the Commission shall have the right—

        (A)   to be heard with respect to any matter that arises in that action; and

        (B)   to file a petition for appeal.

(c) CONSTRUCTION- For purposes of bringing any civil action under subsection (a), nothing in this Act shall be construed to prevent an attorney general of a State from exercising the powers conferred on the attorney general by the laws of that State to—

    (1)   conduct investigations;

    (2)   administer oaths or affirmations; or

    (3)   compel the attendance of witnesses or the production of documentary and other evidence.

(d) ACTIONS BY THE COMMISSION- In any case in which an action is instituted by or on behalf of the Commission for violation of any regulation prescribed under section 3, no State may, during the pendency of that action, institute an action under subsection (a) against any defendant named in the complaint in that action for violation of that regulation.

(e) VENUE; SERVICE OF PROCESS—

    (1)   VENUE—Any action brought under subsection (a) may be brought in the district court of the United States—

        (A)   in which the defendant—

            (i)   is found;

            (ii)   is an inhabitant; or

            (iii)   transacts business; or

        (B)   that otherwise meets applicable requirements relating to venue under section 1391 of title 28, United States Code.

    (2)   SERVICE OF PROCESS- In an action brought under subsection (a), process may be served in any district in which the defendant—

        (A)   is an inhabitant; or

        (B)   may be found.

(f) ACTIONS BY OTHER STATE OFFICIALS—

    (1) IN GENERAL- Nothing in this section may be construed to prohibit a State official from proceeding a court of the State in accordance with the laws of that State on the basis of an alleged violation of any civil or criminal law of that State.

    (2) CERTAIN ACTIONS IN STATE COURTS—In addition to any actions brought by an attorney general of a State under subsection (a), an action described in paragraph (1) may be brought by any other officer of that State who is authorized by the State to bring such an action in that State on behalf of the residents of the State.

SEC. 6. ADMINISTRATION AND APPLICABILITY OF ACT.

(a) IN GENERAL- Except as otherwise provided, this Act shall be enforced by the Commission under the Federal Trade Commission Act (15 U.S.C. 41 et seq.).

(b) PROVISIONS- Compliance with the requirements imposed under this subchapter shall be enforced under—

    (1) section 8 of the Federal Deposit Insurance Act (12 U.S.C. 1818), in the case of—

        (A) national banks, and Federal branches and Federal agencies of foreign banks, by the Office of the Comptroller of the Currency;

        (B) member banks of the Federal Reserve System (other than national banks), branches and agencies of foreign banks (other than Federal branches, Federal agencies, and insured State branches of foreign banks), commercial lending companies owned or controlled by foreign banks, and organizations operating under section 25 or

25(a) of the Federal Reserve Act (12 U.S.C. 601 et seq. and 611 et seq.), by the Board; and

(C)   banks insured by the Federal Deposit Insurance Corporation (other than members of the Federal Reserve System) and insured State branches of foreign banks, by the Board of Directors of the Federal Deposit Insurance Corporation;

(2)   section 8 of the Federal Deposit Insurance Act (12 U.S.C. 1818), by the Director of the Office of Thrift Supervision, in the case of a savings association the deposits of which are insured by the Federal Deposit Insurance Corporation;

(3)   the Federal Credit Union Act (12 U.S.C. 1751 et seq.), by the National Credit Union Administration Board with respect to any Federal credit union;

(4)   part A of subtitle VII of title 49, by the Secretary of Transportation with respect to any air carrier or foreign air carrier subject to that part;

(5)   the Packers and Stockyards Act, 1921 (7 U.S.C. 181 et seq.) (except as provided in section 406 of that Act (7 U.S.C. 226, 227)), by the Secretary of Agriculture with respect to any activities subject to that Act; and

(6)   the Farm Credit Act of 1971 (12 U.S.C. 2001 et seq.) by the Farm Credit Administration with respect to any Federal land bank, Federal land bank association, Federal intermediate credit bank, or production credit association.

(c) EXERCISE OF CERTAIN POWERS- For the purpose of the exercise by any agency referred to in subsection (a) of its powers under any Act referred to in that subsection, a violation of any requirement imposed under this Act shall be deemed to be a violation of a requirement imposed under that Act. In addition to its powers under any provision of law specifically referred to in subsection (a), each of the agencies referred to in that subsection may exercise, for the purpose of enforcing compliance with any requirement imposed under this Act, any other authority conferred on it by law.

(d) ACTIONS BY THE COMMISSION- The Commission shall prevent any person from violating a rule of the Commission under section 3 in the same manner, by the same means, and with the same jurisdiction, powers, and duties as though all applicable terms and provisions of the Federal Trade Commission Act (15 U.S.C. 41 et seq.) were incorporated into and made a part of this Act. Any entity that violates such rule shall be subject to the penalties and entitled to the privileges and immunities provided in the Federal Trade Commission Act in the same manner, by the same means, and with the same jurisdiction, power, and duties as though all applicable terms and provisions of the Federal Trade Commission Act were incorporated into and made a part of this Act.

(e) EFFECT ON OTHER LAWS- Nothing contained in the Act shall be construed to limit the authority of the Commission under any other provisions of law.

SEC. 7. REVIEW.

(a) IN GENERAL—Not later than 5 years after the effective date of the regulations initially issued under section 3, the Commission shall—

    (1) review the implementation of this Act, including the effect of the implementation of this Act on practices relating to the disclosure of information relating to children; and

    (2) prepare and submit to Congress a report the results of the review under paragraph (1).

Appendix Q—
Recommended Reading

Publications

Financial Privacy News. A monthly newsletter detailing all aspects of privacy, offshore banking, and asset protection. Editor: Dr. Styvesant J. Fishdt III 1293 Pavas 1200 Costa Rica or SJO-966, P.O. Box 025216, Miami, FL 33182 Cost $49/Yr. (506) 231-1480 (t/f) Email: stephenw@sol.racsa.co.cr

Full Disclosure. A monthly newspaper on surveillance and civil liberties issues. Editor: Glen Roberts. PO Box 1533, Oil City, PA 16301. Cost: $29.95/year.

Privacy Newsletter. Monthly newsletter that shows consumers how to get privacy and keep it. Shares key privacy stories, abuses, and public attitudes. Provides hope, encouragement, and inspiration to individuals who seek freedom from Big Brother. Editor: John Featherman. E-mail: privacy@mindspring.com. Address: PO Box 8206, Philadelphia PA 19101-8206.

Books

White, Juliette Arlene. *Credit Mechanic: The Poor Man's Guide to Credit Repair.* Boulder, CO.: Paladin Press, 1991

This step-by-step guide is organized in workbook fashion to help you fix your credit yourself, without the help of expensive credit repair clinics. Inside tips on credit repair (some found nowhere else) show you how to turn bureaucracy in your favor and wipe the slate clean for good.

Smith, Robert Ellis et al. *Compilation of State and Federal Privacy Laws*. Providence, RI: Privacy Journal, 1997.

This compilation is a quick reference work on privacy legislation from the Privacy Journal. Published monthly by Robert Ellis Smith, Privacy Journal has been collecting and publishing state and federal privacy laws since 1975. Like its predecessors, this volume contains short summaries by state and by record type of the current legal standing of privacy and data protection.

Regan, Priscilla M. *Legislating Privacy: Technology, Social Values, and Public Policy*. University of North Carolina Press, 1995

Assistant Professor of Political Science at George Mason University and former technology-society expert at the U.S. Office of Technology Assessment, Priscilla Regan provides an excellent review of privacy-related writings and case studies of successful and unsuccessful privacy legislation.

Cate, Fred H. *Privacy in the Information Age*
Brookings Institute, 1997

Indiana University Law Professor Fred Cate has produced an important synthesis of law review literature, court cases, legislation, political thought, and recent works on privacy.

Dale Fetherling, Dale (Editor). *The Privacy Rights Handbook: How to Take Control of Your Personal Information*. New York: Avon Books, 1997.

Beth Givens has written a consumer-oriented guide for those who want to regain control of their personal information.

Rothfeder, Jeffrey. *Privacy For Sale*. New York: Simon & Schuster, 1992.

An examination of the world of information takes readers on a guided tour of the big three credit agencies, demonstrating why privacy laws are hopelessly outdated and what people can do to minimize their invasions of privacy.

Skousen, Mark. *Complete Guide to Financial Privacy*. Alexandria, VA: Alexandria House, 1982.

Glossary

Bad faith. Intent to deceive. A person who intentionally tries to deceive or mislead another in order to gain some advantages.

Children's Online Privacy Protection Act. A federal law requiring that parents be notified and required to give their consent before any information is collected from children.

Consumer Credit Code. A uniform law, adopted by several states, with intent and purpose similar to that of the federal Consumer Credit Protection Act.

Consumer Credit Protection Act. A federal law requiring the clear disclosure of consumer credit (see that word) information by companies making loans or selling on credit. The act requires that finance charges (see that word) be expressed as a standard annual percentage rate (APR), gives consumers the right to back out of certain deals, regulates credit cards, restricts wage garnishments, etc. It is also called the Truth-in-Lending Act. Many states have adopted legislation similar to the federal act.

Consumer credit. Money, property, or services offered to a person for personal, family, or household purposes "on time." It is "consumer credit" if there is a finance charge or if there are more than four installment payments.

Consumer. A person who buys (or rents, travels on, or uses) something for personal, rather than business use.

Conversion Any act that deprives an owner of property without that owner's permission and without just cause. For example, it is conversion to refuse to return a borrowed book.

Cookie. A text file saved in your browser's directory or folder and stored in RAM while your browser is running.

Credit bureau. A place that keeps records on the credit used by persons and on their financial reliability.

Credit inquiry. An attempt to seek information concerning interest rates and the availability of funds without disclosing your identity, or specifying the need or purpose of the proposed borrowing, or the specifics concerning your creditworthiness.

Credit line. (see *line of credit*).

Credit rating. The evaluation of a person's or businesses' ability and past performance in paying debts. A credit rating is generally established by a credit bureau and used by merchants, suppliers, and bankers to determine whether a loan should be granted or credit extended.

Debit card. A plastic card that allows a person to make a purchase that is paid for by a direct subtraction from the person's bank account. It looks like a credit card but works like a check.

Deceit. A fraudulent misrepresentation or contrivance, by which one man deceives another, who has no
deduction, exemption, and exclusion.

Disclosure. Revealing something that is secret or not well understood. For example, the disclosure in a patent application is the statement of what the invention is, what it does, and how it works. In consumer law, disclosure refers to what information must be made available in a loan or other credit deal and how that information must be presented to make it clear.

Dumpster diving. The active rummaging through trash cans, dumpsters at apartment complexes and behind shopping centers for personal and business data.

Equal Credit Opportunity Act. A federal law prohibiting discrimination based on race, color, religion, sex, national origin, or age in any credit transaction.

Federal Trade Commission. Agency of the federal government created in 1914. Its main functions are to promote free and fair competition in interstate commerce through prohibitions against unfair competition in business and "unfair or deceptive acts or trade practices."

Federal Privacy Act of 1974. Federal law permitting an individual to have access to records containing personal information and allows the individual to control the transfer of that information to other Federal agencies for nonroutine uses.

Fair Credit Billing Act. A federal law regulating billing disputes and making credit card companies partially responsible for items bought by consumers.

Fair Credit Reporting Acts. Federal and state laws regulating the organizations that investigate, store, and give out consumer credit information, organizations that collect bills, etc. Consumers are given rights to know about investigations, see and dispute their files, etc.

False Impersonation of a citizen. 18, U.S.C., 911, makes it a Federal crime or offense for anyone to falsely and willfully impersonate a citizen of the United States.

False Pretences. False representations and statements, made with a fraudulent design, to obtain " money, goods,

Falsehood. A willful act or declaration contrary to truth. It is committed either by the willful act of the party, by dissimulation, or by words. It's willful for example, when the owner of a thing sells it twice by different contracts to different individuals, unknown to them; for in this the seller must willfully declare the thing is his own when he knows that it is not so.

Forgery. Making a fake document (or altering a real one) with intent to commit a fraud.

Fraud. A knowing misrepresentation made with intent of causing another to rely upon it to the latter's detriment.

Identity theft. The stealing of someone's identity (i.e., your name, birth date or Social Security Number).

Intent to defraud. The specific intent to deceive or cheat, ordinarily for the purpose of causing some financial loss to another, or bringing about some financial gain to one's self. It is not necessary, however, to prove that the United States or anyone else was in fact defrauded so long as it is established that the person acted "with intent to defraud."

Line of credit. The promise to lend money up to a certain maximum that a merchant or bank will give to a customer, usually for an ongoing series of transactions.

Misrepresentation. The statement made by a party to a contract, that a thing relating to it is in fact in a particular way, when he knows it is not so.

Privacy. Describes the right to be left alone. The right to privacy is sometimes "balanced" against other rights, such as freedom of the press.

Social Security Administration. A federal agency, set up by the Social Security Act and the Federal Insurance Contribution Act (FICA), that administers a national Old Age, Survivors, and Disability Insurance program and other insurance and welfare programs.

Statute of frauds. Any of various state laws, modeled after an old English law, that require many types of contracts (such as contracts for the sale of real estate and certain long-term contracts) to be signed and in writing to be enforceable in court. wares, and merchandise " with intent to cheat.

Index